Twayne's English Authors Series

EDITOR OF THIS VOLUME

Kinley E. Roby

Northeastern University

George Moore

TEAS 244

GEORGE MOORE

By ANTHONY FARROW

Saint Bonaventure University

TWAYNE PUBLISHERS
A Division of G. K. Hall & Co.
Boston, Massachusetts, U.S.A.

Copyright © 1978 by G.K. Hall & Co.
Published in 1978 by Twayne Publishers,
A Division of G. K. Hall & Co.
All Rights Reserved

Printed on permanent/durable acid-free paper and bound
in the United States of America

First Printing

Frontispiece photo of George Moore

Library of Congress Cataloging in Publication Data

Farrow, Anthony.
George Moore.

(Twayne's English authors series ; TEAS 244)
Bibliography: p. 163–67
Includes index.
1. Moore, George, 1852–1933—Criticism and interpretation.
PR5044.F3   823'.8   78-19041
ISBN 0-8057-6685-5

Contents

About the Author

Preface

Chronology

1. Life and Influences   11

2. Early Writings   22

3. Ambitions and Experiments   52

4. O To Be In Ireland   103

5. Last Novels   138

    Notes and References   161

    Selected Bibliography   163

    Index   167

About the Author

Anthony Farrow was born in England in 1944 and educated in England, Canada, and the United States, receiving his B.A. from the University of Toronto and his M.A. and Ph.D. from Cornell University. He is currently assistant professor of English at Saint Bonaventure University. In addition to articles and reviews on Modern British literature, Professor Farrow is the editor of *Diarmuid and Grania* by George Moore and W. B. Yeats (1974). Currently at work on a book on Samuel Beckett, Professor Farrow is married to Elvira Farrow, herself the author of a book and many articles on Montessori education.

Preface

In his long career George Moore produced a body of work remarkable for its quality, its bulk, and its varied interest. It is the aim of the present volume to fasten upon the first of these, to examine the quality of Moore as a writer, to perform an act of critical retrieval which will examine the works as self-consistent artistic units, linked only by the sustaining patterns of their creator's mind.

In the past there has been no lack of interest in the aspects of Moore's life and writing habits which shed light on his incorporation of the ideas and practice of Émile Zola or on his involvement with experiments in England's independent noncommercial theater, or on his enthusiasm for work of Walter Pater. But while such investigations are of great importance, they are not perhaps directed at the question of internal consistency which is central to the important issues of artistic achievement.

At present much of the work of George Moore is out of print and often difficult and expensive to obtain. This situation is improving somewhat, with perhaps a half dozen books available through publishers at the present time. Moore's one unqualified commercial success, *Esther Waters*, has rarely been out of print since its first publication, but even here critical evaluation has been severely hampered by alarming misreadings by its admirers (while its detractors have consistently judged it in terms quite irrelevant to the actual features of its achievement). ·Without seeming too paradoxical, it is possible to argue that *Esther Waters* is the most misunderstood of Moore's books, despite its apparent popularity. This evidence of the lack of appreciation for the most familiar of his novels suggests that there is need for an examination of his total output in terms of his quality of workmanship.

The approach taken here is a generally chronological study of many of George Moore's works from his early poetry to his late novels. All of the major novels have been considered, but there has been no attempt at comprehensiveness. The emphasis, as in Moore's own case, is chiefly on the fiction, although discussions of the poetry and the dramatic work have been introduced wherever they seemed able to provide helpful information for the consideration of the novels or short stories. Because of the chronological interest in Moore's development as a writer, analysis has been restricted only to the first edition of each work, since the earliest forms of the novels provide the best clue to Moore's intentions at the time.

It is not possible to discuss such a complex writer as George Moore without some reference to the many other writers reflected in his work, either by imitation or allusion; but these influences have not been included in separate chapters. Instead such discussion has been incorporated into the analysis of particular novels in order to shed light on the text as it seems fitting. For detailed consideration of influences on Moore's work or fuller biographical information or studies of textual revisions the reader is referred to the works cited in the bibliography.

Any writer is inevitably in debt to his predecessors. I take this opportunity to acknowledge the fine examples of scholarship in the field, and to announce a special gratitude to Edwin Gilcher, Phillip L. Marcus, and Thomas D. Hill.

Chronology

1852　George Augustus Moore born on 24 February at Moore Hall, County Mayo, son of George Henry Moore and Mary (Blake) Moore.

1861　Sent to school at St. Mary's, Oscott, in England; course of studies never completed.

1869　Moore family moves to London. George makes unimpressive showing as a student of art at the South Kensington Museum.

1870　Death of George Henry Moore.

1873　George Moore moves to Paris. Enrolls in art classes at the Beaux Arts and the Salon Jullian.

1878　Ideas of painting now abandoned. Appearance of first book of poetry. *Flowers of Passion.*

1880　Leaves Paris for London.

1883　Appearance of first novel, *A Modern Lover.*

1888　Publication of *Confessions of a Young Man.*

1894　Publication of *Esther Waters.*

1901　Moves to Dublin. Peak of collaboration in Irish Renaissance.

1903　Appearance of *The Untilled Field.*

1911　Moves to London. Appearance of first part of *Hail and Farewell.*

1916　Appearance of *The Brook Kerith.*

1921　Appearance of *Heloise and Abelard.*

1933　Appearance of *A Communication to My Friends.* Novelist's death, January 22.

CHAPTER 1

Life and Influences

I Childhood and Education

GEORGE Augustus Moore was born on February 24, 1852, the heir to twelve thousand acres and a large, well-situated house. He was the last of several generations of Irish landlords, all known for their willfulness, a trait which, along with a certain degree of personal and financial shrewdness, the novelist was to inherit. The mysteries of ancestry are hard to penetrate, but it seems reasonable to assume that at least some of the opinions and habits possessed by Moore at maturity can be traced to his early years. The arguments that were to be hurled against formalized education in art during the years of his art criticism are traceable not only to the failure that followed his experiences in the School of Art in the South Kensington Museum and his deplorable showing earlier as a schoolboy at St. Mary's, Oscott, but also to the career of his father, who, although a competent and even distinguished student, was sufficiently stubborn to learn with ease only what he chose to learn.

George Henry Moore, the father who said of his sons George and Maurice "I fear those two redheaded boys are stupid" (a fear eventually proved groundless, since all four Moore boys achieved a level of attainment far above the average), was himself a figure of considerable prominence in his time. His early successes at St. Mary's were not followed by a happy course of studies at Cambridge, where he spent too much of his time racing and hunting, pastimes which reveal a strain of recklessness in the Moore family best seen in the conduct of George Henry Moore's brother Augustus, killed in a racing accident, or in his uncle John Moore, the rebel President of the Republic of Connaught. Brought into conflict with his parents through an affair with a married woman, George Henry, as his son

11

was often to do, sought to solve his problems with a change of locale, and escaped to the Middle East, where he captured his recollections in a series of notebooks and drawings which betray a keen power of observation.

After his inheritance of the estate George Henry returned to racing, an interest in which he prospered in general until the Irish famine of the 1840s forced him to sell his horses. Like his supposedly cold-hearted son he refused to drive out tenants who were farming impracticably small holdings, a gesture which earned him not only gratitude for his humanity, but enough votes in the 1847 election to win a parliamentary seat for Mayo. Thereafter his parliamentary career was interrupted at least once, and the gap filled with a resumption of horse-racing; but his interest in politics remained constant until his death in 1870. Despite appreciable gifts as a public speaker and undoubted courage, George Henry Moore lacked political sense—taken in both its cynical and its common significance as an ability to trust and compromise with others—and his fiery independence was as much a liability as an advantage in nineteenth-century statecraft. A man in favor of Repeal of the Union, he soon fell out with those of his class whose interests were naturally more conservative, but as time went on he also found himself unable to tolerate the later breed of Nationalists seeking land reform to a degree unacceptable to a member of parliament who was, after all, an Irish landlord. When his own tenants refused to pay their rents in 1870, he determined to return to Ireland and deal with them sternly; but in fact he died within a few days of his return. The peculiar blend of political acuteness and stubbornness in the face of inevitable social fact which was to find its way into young George Moore's *Parnell and his Island* unquestionably takes its origin from the experiences of the father's political life; and it is likely from his father, too, that the writer learned to equate personal ability with self-will of an almost perverse intensity.

As a boy, the novelist did not impress his parents with his capacities, as has been seen. Late and fumbling in his acquisition of the power of speech, he paid little attention to his governess. For his parents to send him to Oscott College at the age of nine was almost an act of desperation. From the beginning he was unhappy, and this fact alone perhaps suffices to explain his abysmal performance in Latin and French, subjects in which he appears to have known less after four years at Oscott than the year he left Mayo.

Oscar Wilde, then also a boy, used to spend his summers in Mayo; his superiority in matters of learning and articulateness is possibly the source of Moore's lifelong animosity toward him. At any event, the sad experiment of sending the boy to Oscott was plainly a failure signalled most strongly, perhaps, by the headmaster's written opinion that of George's general proficiency he could not say too little—this accompanied by a remarkable and ingenious sample of a number of the boy's spelling errors taken from within the same sentence. In 1867 young Moore was brought home.

The memories of Oscott were sufficiently painful that years later, the novelist, usually the possessor of a clear memory, was forced to rely upon his brother to supply even quite significant facts about the period. Near the end of his stay he managed to shock the other boys by the intensity of his attraction for a servant girl: here the scandal was incidental, but in his admiration for the heterodox Shelley and in his consequent loud profession of atheism he was indulging a very strong inclination to tread on conventional corns, for the desire to shock was deliberate. Repeating the experiment at Moore Hall, the boy was chagrined that his parents were not outwardly moved at the prospect of an atheist in the family, but were rendered considerably ill at ease by his suggestion of becoming a jockey. The election of 1869 necessitated the removal of the Moore family to London where the future novelist, now eighteen years old, amended his ambitions to the point of seeking to become a bettor rather than a rider of horses, and did, in fact, enjoy a moderate success in this interest. The question of a career for the future heir now became a matter of urgent, though not very helpful discussion. A term of art school in Kensington was followed by a course of studies with an army tutor, but in neither institution did George give satisfaction, and it was only his father's death that freed him from the burdens of education. Although a minor, he was now the head of the family and master of his destiny, which he had decided must take the form of a painter's life in Paris.

II *Paris and Early Writings*

In March of 1873 George Moore arrived in Paris ready to do whatever was required in order to be an artist, though it appears that he did not at the time consider this profession incompatible with the manner of an Irish landlord, since he brought with him a lamentably home-sick man-servant named William Moloney. (Indeed, in many ways Moore never relinquished his native Feudal-lordship. One can detect in the Paris years the substitution of the hauteur of art for the distinction of property; even as an elderly man-of-letters the novelist consciously indulged a pose of aristo-cracy in his literary position.) After several fruitless attempts to find a painter who would take him as a pupil, Moore was able to find a place in the studio of M. Jullian, a man whose previous career as shepherd and circus masked man anticipated the wandering search for vocation of many characters to be seen later in Moore's novels. It was at the Salon Jullian that Moore first met Lewis Weldon Haw-kins, first introduced in terms of his Irish connections, but with his fluency, his plausibility, and his utter lack of personal talent des-tined to be the very type of the failed artist to be depicted again and again: Marshall in *Confessions of a Young Man* is Hawkins; Lewis Seymour in *A Modern Lover* is very like him; even the portrait of Yeats in *Hail and Farewell* has a tincture of this acquaintance who succeeded generally in maintaining only the public appearance of artistic vigor.

Moore accepted Hawkins as a flat-mate, actually as a rent-free lodger; but although the arrangement lasted for some time it was not profitable in terms of immediate artistic attainment, for during this period Moore came to realize that he would never be a painter. In 1876 he began what was to be the first of many dramatic collabora-tions, this time with Bernard Lopez, a writer whose list of previous partners in art would furnish a history of nineteenth-century French literature—Théophile Gautier, Dumas père, Augustin Scribe, and others. The finished play, *Martin Luther,* was not published for some time, and it was never performed, yet it released a hidden psychic spring, since it was at this time that Moore determined to become a professional writer. The play turned out to be uneven and derivative, as were the poems that Moore began to collect for publi-cation in two volumes, *Flowers of Passion* and *Pagan Poems,* and that the critics received with stiffly phrased malice. This, however, did not succeed in discouraging the young author. By the time his first novel, *A Modern Lover,* appeared, Moore had already found his great central theme of choice of vocation, usually the artist's, and begun to develop the notion that success in art or life is not a matter of talent, still less of luck, so much as an application of certain qualities of character to the available experiences in a milieu.

The choice of Paris had obviously been a fateful one for the young man of 1873, but in moving to London seven years later Moore, now twenty-eight, was taking the substance, not merely the show, of artistic life, because with the reduction of income caused by difficulties in Ireland he was forced to support himself by his pen and devote all of his time to his craft. *A Modern Lover* was not a financial success or a critical one either, and came close to being an economic disaster for the already-straitened writer until a fire at his publisher's warehouse saved him from the necessity of making up the loss due to poor sales. Not a single one of his books had promised a secure fiscal or—candidly—artistic return, but *A Modern Lover* brought complications of another kind, for the circulating libraries which then controlled the book trade emphatically declined to handle what they saw as a prurient novel. In France Moore had been able to encourage his lively impulse to cast scorn on the mob of pious and conventional souls; it was perhaps inevitable that he should regard this affront not only as an assault on his purse but as an attack upon art itself. In the years to come he waged a vigorous and effective war against the circulating libraries, though it is now impossible to decide how much of the successful campaign was due to his efforts, the foolishness of the policies of the libraries, or internal changes within the publishing industry itself.

For such a stubbornly self-willed figure as he everywhere proved himself to be, Moore was a writer capable of momentary enthusiasms for other writers and movements, as his otherwise inexplicable involvement in the Irish Renaissance at the turn of the century shows. In the early 1880s Moore's enthusiasm was for Émile Zola, a writer whom he had known in Paris and who was to have considerable immediate effect, though little permanent influence beyond a shared interest in unstable characters whose reaction to environment is always problematic. Zola suggested that if Moore were to publish a successful one-volume novel in a cheap format, the power of the circulating libraries might be counteracted (the advice was good, but to make such a demand of a writer as monumentally unpopular as George Moore was at the time evidences a capacity for hope of inspiring proportions). *A Mummer's Wife*, when it appeared, was a fine book and taken at the time as a Naturalistic novel marking the interest in French literature among English writers. George Bernard Shaw, who did not read the work, considered it a sufficient reason for his reluctance to believe he was ignoring a masterpiece to say merely that he knew George Moore; but among critics of favorable and unfavorable parties there was no doubt of the book's importance: a new and highly distinctive, if somewhat abrasive, voice had arrived on the London literary scene.

Yet even at the moment of being decisively linked with Zola and Naturalism Moore was coming under the influence of other, and far different minds. Thereafter, although decreasing dosages of Naturalism can be detected in a A Drama in Muslin, A Mere Accident, and the sequence of novels which lead up to Esther Waters, Moore showed a growing interest in the rendering of psychological rather than simply physical events. The two commonly cited sources of this shift of allegiance are Walter Pater and Ivan Turgenev; and indeed there can be no doubt of Moore's admiration for these writers, although his discovery of the French writer Édouard Dujardin is perhaps of greater significance. But Moore had always cared for what he felt about the hard facts of experience rather than for facts themselves; his early interest in autobiography and disguised autobiography as the central core of his work is arguably the best reason for his search for a form that might capture the elusive substance of mental existence. That he succeeded is to be seen in the generally accepted view that the direct line of descent of the stream-of-consciousness technique used by such writers as James Joyce goes back to George Moore before it diffuses into the various influences of Dujardin, Richard Wagner, the Bible, and elsewhere.

Certainly in the charming and garrulous memoirs of Confessions of a Young Man Moore has departed hugely from the precedent of Zola, who, in fact, is singled out for mild censure in the pages of that book. By the time Esther Waters was published in 1894, the novelist was ready with a novel that challenged the central Naturalist thesis of the primacy of environment with its story of a heroine who achieves her stature precisely by challenging the conditions of her life. The philosopher Schopenhauer is often proposed as the fountainhead of this notion in Moore's work that what counts most of all in life is the quality of the individual soul; but apart from some obvious debts to the German in the formulation of the idea, it is probably aboriginal with Moore, given his disposition.

III   Later Career

Two things distinguish George Moore throughout his long career, his impressionability and his retentiveness, characteristics seemingly contradictory but actually the key to his personality. Living for some seven years in France and for a much longer period in England, Moore the Irish landlord did not cease to be himself but was absorbed by the boulevardier, the prolific London literary figure, the distinguished art critic, finally by the white-haired Panjandrum of Chelsea. A consequence of this rule is that although the past was frequently modified (and in the autobiographies judged or chuckled over), it was never entirely discarded. In the 1880s Moore had written two books on Irish subjects, *A Drama in Muslin* and *Parnell and his Ireland,* which almost qualify this time to be known as Moore's first Irish period. He saw in Ireland a fit theme for literary quarrying as well as a hopeless case of retrograde social and religious malaise. *A Drama in Muslin* frames its concluding vision of the general squalor of the country in an apparently gratuitous hope that this is, after all, the inevitable decay that must precede an outburst of national energy. This was in 1886, a time when most Irish landlords had had enough outbursts of energy directed at them in the troubles of the preceding decade, and a moment at which few people were prepared to believe that Ireland had any kind of future.

The kind of outburst Moore contemplated, of course, was cultural, perhaps artistic, and when he heard six years later from his cousin, Edward Martyn, that there was a great revival of interest in the Irish language and in writing literature in Irish (a tongue with which the novelist had the most distant kind of familiarity), he was immediately enthusiastic, though not in a way that precipitated his own entry into the movement. Nevertheless, he had always maintained his Irish contacts and appears to have known most of the Irish writers in London, including, from the early 1890s onwards, the poet W. B. Yeats. In particular Moore admired Yeat's *The Celtic Twilight,* an 1893 collection of stories which was to have some influence on his own later stories in *The Untilled Field;* Yeats's later collection *The Secret Rose* was also valued, as were his early lyrics.

Acquaintance ripened into active collaboration in the play *Diarmuid and Grania,* not to be completed until 1901, and it was probably from Yeats that Moore acquired his first detailed knowledge of Irish mythology and folklore, knowledge which was to provide a useful store of fictional materials for many years to come. Yeats appears as a character in the 1898 novel *Evelyn Innes,* in which an idealistic, poetic, and rather ineffectual young man named Ulick Dean obviously represents the poet in Moore's conception of the time. Ulick is writing an opera, "Grania," based on the same legend

that Yeats was recounting to Moore at the time as the basis of their
play, and, as will be seen, the treatment of certain details of plot and
character in *Evelyn Innes* owes something to Moore's familiarity
with the Irish source. At the early stages of his relationship with
Yeats, however, it is clear that Moore was comparatively detached
in his attitude to the Irish Renaissance—both pleased that new Irish
materials were being excavated which could be of service to a
sophisticated novelist in a distant London house, and convinced, at
the same time, that Ireland had not changed, that peasants were still
peasants and priests, priests.

From the late 1880s Moore had been interested in experimenting
in England with some equivalent of the *Théatre Libre* in France; he
wanted a small semiprivate company free from commercial pressures and free to put on works selected only on the basis of artistic
merit. It is doubtful if any such organization has ever flourished in
England despite the many letters and articles published by Moore
and others throughout the late eighties and early nineties; but the
idea has a notable similarity to that possessed by those who gave
birth to the various groups destined to become the Abbey Theatre.
Finding his cousin Edward Martyn and his acquaintance W. B.
Yeats already committed to such an idea, but without much dramatic experience themselves, Moore consented to become a third
director of the Irish Literary Theatre, a group sustained by the ideas
and skills of Yeats and Moore—and by an appreciable amount of
money from Martyn. Yeats and Moore were destined to quarrel
about the selection of actors, methods of performance, the theatrical
program, about everything that touched upon the conduct of the
theater. Yet it was none of these problems nor the formidable interposition of Lady Gregory that caused Moore's withdrawal from this
venture so much as the enormous amounts of time that had to be
spent satisfying a generally hostile public unsympathetic to the aims
of the whole scheme. Not at all averse to controversy, the novelist
was not ready for the sustained squabbling necessary for the
maintenance of any artistic project in Ireland. Yeats alone of the
three proved to have the dogged patience demanded at the time and
long afterwards, and, as all the world knows, the achievements of
twentieth-century Irish drama are due principally to him.

Ever a loner, Moore now used his home in Dublin as a base from
which to stalk the wild Gael, to observe the behavior of the beast,

and to cast scornful aspersions on its general quality. Even during the few years between 1896 and 1902 when he was generally enthusiastic about the Irish Renaissance, he had been very plain of speech about the necessity of freeing Ireland from its clerical slavery: in reality all that separates the generally optimistic first edition of *The Untilled Field,* Moore's collection of Irish short stories, from its generally pessimistic successors is the realization that such an emancipation is impossible in Ireland. *The Untilled Field* contains many stories of narrow and oppressive priests, narrow and oppressed peasants, and free and vigorous men and women whose only response to clerical tyranny is to leave the country as soon as they can. In the next book, *The Lake,* Moore dwells upon another priest, who gains consciousness of himself much as Edwin Dayne did in *Confessions of a Young Man;* but here this acquisition of lucidity requires that the priest abandon his vocation and his country at the same time, for exile and the search for life have become almost synonymous.

Hail and Farewell, the last book attempted before Moore's return to London (in fact it was concluded in England), continues the same theme, since Moore intended it with only a partial smile as a "Holy Book" to convert the Irish from their long clerical hibernation. In fact an account of his stay in Ireland complete with names, dates, and malicious opinions, it is Moore's longest and most daring work, conceived on the scale of the autobiographies of Augustine and Rousseau and arguably the finest work of autobiography in English. In a series of brilliant portraits of the major figures of the Irish Renaissance Moore reduces to the concrete particular his general argument that in its Church-inspired fear of normal sexuality Irish experience is deficient in the appreciation of life—Yeats, Martyn, and George Russell are ultimately judged deficient as men and as artists because there is something essential missing in their approach to existence. Modern libel laws render it unlikely that such a penetrating and sustained critique of living human beings could be published in Great Britain today, but the real butt of the account is made to be that naive and impressionable George Moore who was so foolish as to believe in the possibility of art in Ireland. There seemed to be an operative law in Moore's life that momentary enthusiasms must be repented of and paid for with the retrospective sackcloth of autobiography. *Hail and Farewell* is a penance for an excess of credulity in the supposition that anything good could come from his native land.

When the third volume of *Hail and Farewell* appeared Moore was already sixty years old; the novelist had almost twenty years of writing left to him, but critics have found it too easy to explain the markedly different quality of his last work by pointing to the declining energy of an elderly man. Even if this view is accepted, and with it the undoubtedly true proposition that in old age Moore enjoyed a position of man-of-letters that was not good for him, important qualities of his work in this period are not so easily explained. It seems to be beyond reasonable argument, for example, that the famous "melodic line" of the later novels is a matter of conscious choice and experiment, influenced probably by the work of Walter Pater and Irish oral literature, but not in the least the result of the unfocussing sensibilities of someone facing the final test of life. Rolling on and on, sometimes lasting for a page or longer, the sentences of his latest style were the logical consequence of years of development in Moore's writing. Impressed through Dujardin by the success of Wagner in combining all the various effects of opera by the use of motif, Moore, too, wanted to make his novels "all melody" in the sense of making the unit of composition, here the sentence, also the basic unit of structure. This, at least, was his intent; opinion is notably divided on whether he succeeded.

These later works—*The Brook Kerith, Héloise and Abelard, Ulick and Soracha, Aphrodite in Aulis*—are also Moore's best-knit narratives, although the seamless form is perhaps achieved at the cost of simplifying materials to an almost ethereal condition. An interest in historical re-creation pervades all of them, an interest once again characteristic of an elderly man, no doubt, but still one cognate to Moore's lifelong interest in delineating the precise tints and tones present in various cultures and conditions of life from Mayo to Montmartre. Of their nature such works were never intended for a wide audience; issued originally in limited editions they enjoyed a small but dependable sale, yet even now one frequently comes across a fifty-year-old first edition by Moore with no signs or marks to indicate a complete reading.

As a youth in London Moore might have been an acquaintance of Anthony Trollope, had he chosen; Dante Rossetti he did know, and

Algernon Swinburne and William Morris; yet he lived through decades that were to see the rise of James Joyce, Virginia Woolf, T. S. Eliot, Franz Kafka, even the early Samuel Beckett. It was a career that saw prodigious changes, many of them, when he died in January, 1933, traceable to George Moore himself.

CHAPTER 2

Early Writings

I The Poetry

IF quality were the only consideration, then one would have to put George Moore's poetry with Winston Churchill's painting, Isaac Newton's alchemy, and George Bernard Shaw's novels as the innocuous diversions of a mind whose peculiar abilities obviously lie elsewhere. Having found his home in fiction, Moore later refused to treat his poetry as more than apprentice work or part of the mine of autobiographical materials which could be used in his novels. And yet these poems, derivative as they often are, show a consistent point of view toward their subjects, even when these subjects are not otherwise clearly delineated; their lack of technical command does not altogether impede the authority of their vision.

Moore was only twenty-six years old when *Flowers of Passion* was published in a cover decorated with a lyre and a skull and crossbones at the author's expense. Perhaps twenty-six was not so young for the first book of a lyric poet, but then Moore had already survived his brief life as a painter before thinking of a career in literature; and this book with its swaggering cover reads like a young man's effort. Certainly the English reviewers were put off by the bluster of its general tone and by suspicions of unnamed depravities lurking for the virtuous reader. One critic suggested that the author should be whipped at the cart's tail and his book burned by the hangman. A Gaelic combativeness led Moore to enjoy, and in a certain sense to encourage, this controversy; but he withdrew his book under advice, nursing a grudge against the critical establishment which he was to indulge in great and little battles for years to come.

Moore loved to shock: his delight in the Parisian artistic credo, *épater le bourgeois,* to knock down the philistine, is evident in

Flowers of Passion, with its references to forbidden love—les-
bianism, love of a sister, hints of necrophilia, unorthodox comparisons between nuns and prostitutes. Yet these examinations of exotic
behavior rarely betray any sympathy for, or profound understanding
of, the sexually or morally perverse. Rather, the book is too plainly
the result of insistent literary influences from Rossetti in England
and some half-digested and ill-understood lessons from Charles
Baudelaire and others in France. From Catulle Mendès Moore
came into contact with the works of François Villon, and although he
never achieved the steely simplicity of the original, he was to remain entranced with the experience, deriving the plot of his short
story "The Window" some thirty years later from Villon's "painted
paradise." All his life Moore evinced admiration for poet Algernon
Swinburne: the suspicion might be entertained that at least some of
the Irishman's familiarity with French literature came through the
mediacy of Swinburne, who thus in part occupied the position held
by Arthur Symons later as a bridge between English and French
literature. In any event, some of the more obvious paradoxes re-
sulting from the attractiveness of prohibited behavior stem more
directly from Swinburne than from Baudelaire.

Most of the preoccupations of the thirty-one poems in the collection are to be found in the dedicatory sonnet, which introduces the
motif hinted in the title, "Pale passion flowers I bring to thee my
sweet," a motif explained by the double meaning of the word "passion." Suffering is but the obverse of voluptuous pleasure: here
phrases recalling Christ's Passion—"bitter as frothing of blood," "no
greater gifts"—as well as the traditional symbolism of the passion
flower itself manifest what will be a conspicuous idea in all Moore's
later writing about religious experience. For Moore, religious dedication is the logical equivalent of sexual abandonment. The nun who
takes a wedding ring at her vows is relating herself to Christ in a way
explicitly sexual, just as any woman who commits herself to a man
but in the former case the period of engagement is more protracted.
Other images of religious sacrifice continue this reflection and link it
to the idea that love is not only suffering but a threat to the integrity
of the suffering self. In all this there is the implication that the love
affair, now long dead, is chiefly of present value as the subject of
verse: the implied personal tone in the title "To L—" suggests that
an unhappy experience has been redeemed by artistic translation. It
is, in fact, this promise of the later autobiographer coupled with the

strong, complicated imagery and not any delicacy of language which gives the poem whatever interest it possesses.

"Ode to a Dead Body," the next poem, concerns the view of the corpse of a harlot. The title sounds Baudelairean, but the treatment lacks the irony and unsentimentality of Baudelaire; indeed, the pathetic emotions aroused at the contemplation of the scene suggest the English Romantics. Moore's early fascination with Shelley might account for the emphasis laid upon death as the withering but equivocal conclusion of life both for the harlot and for the nun.

George Moore remained a Romantic all his life in that for him experience itself remained an absolute value; many of his novels deal with the struggle of the central character to free himself from threatening rules or stifling cultural norms. In the much longer "Ginevra," a verse drama and therefore Moore's first play, the same themes are considered at greater length. Antonio confesses to his friend Orisino that he loves his own sister, whereupon Orisino acts like a mid-Victorian journalist: "Have I gone mad, or do I hear aright?"

Antonio's passion and Orisino's outrage at this point together make up the opposing salients of a discussion often of interest to Moore in his later work, in which there are frequently matched pairs of debaters on such topics (Owen Asher and Evelyn Innes in *Evelyn Innes;* Mike Fletcher and John Norton in *Mike Fletcher;* George and Maurice Moore in *Hail and Farewell*). It is important to see that Moore's openness on this point comes not from a personal tolerance he did not in his own life possess, but from a genuine cultural relativism which had far different sources. Antonio argues that if we knew the truth about the meaning of life "we might drink of joy and call life pleasure"; that, in other words, any sense of well-being in a course of behavior is vitiated by a general doubt as to the applicability of all rules of conduct. These liminal questions on life and death pursue Moore's characters for the rest of his career, and they are questions that arise from a primeval experience of the problematic nature of life itself rather than from the frequently invoked examples of Schopenhauer, Pater, or Swinburne, important as such influences may be.

Antonio's sister, Genevra, who becomes a nun, is already a predecessor of Sister Teresa and Héloïse in the fiction of Moore. She looks forward to death and heaven because "the thirst unassuaged yet unsloken/ Will be drowned in the fiercest delight," thus giving utterance to two paradoxes: that the renunciation of sensuality is nevertheless a keen and lasting form of voluptuousness; and that those who claim to be most certain about the value of life are the ones most prone to cast it away. Her preference for the changeless world after death and her consequent disgust with the ephemera of passing events conflict directly with Antonio's feeling of the oddness of the death that is in all things. An interesting discussion seems to be in the offing, but through the necessity of some Elizabethan stage convention Antonio is stabbed by Orisino before a conclusion is reached. In truth there is no fitting subject for dramatic or poetic development here in a purely theoretical argument; still there *is* the germ of a novel or long short story with the proper testing of incident against psychological insight such as Moore was to devise in *Celibates*.

Quite often these poems are unsatisfactory to the extent that the compression of form has left out the things that would be of the greatest interest in a longer narrative. In "Bernice," for example, the speaker is bathing by night with Bernice in a fountain, but a passion comes upon him and drives him to kill her. Motivation, which would most give shape to this splendidly murky act, is unaccountably ignored, with the result that the event has the ludicrous inconsequentiality of a newspaper atrocity. Again, in "Sonnet: Night Perfume," the concluding line, "I lay my head, and dream that love is death," can presumably mean one or both of two things. Either love is frightening, or love is attractive. It must be said that these very interesting ideas are nowhere resolved or clearly articulated (this is a pity, because the notions apparent relate to the belief, found elsewhere in Moore, that love can be a threat to the free experience of life).

"Sonnet: To a Lost Art" is plainly the account of Moore's farewell to painting. There is more than a conventional metaphor in the comparison of art to vainly wooed mistress, for it becomes a commonplace in Moore's novels that love is a natural analogue for art with its total dedication and demands for enormous energy; this also leads to the corollary, often emphasized, that in practice no man can successfully devote himself both to the service of his art and to the full-time pursuit of women. Perhaps even more interesting is the significance of the adjective "weak" in the description of the failed career as a "child of my weak heart." The almost neurotic diligence of Moore's writing habits is perfectly consistent with this early declaration that the essential quality of any artist is a certain aptitude of character. A long series of novels dealing with unsuccessful or incompetent artists and writers (*A Modern Lover, Spring Days, Mike Fletcher, Vain Fortune*) develops from a perception that without strength of will no artistic gift of whatever intensity can take root and grow to maturity.

Strength of will is often little distinguishable from mere stubbornness. A reception such as that accorded to *Flowers of Passion* would have discouraged another man of equal talent and less obstinacy; within three years Moore had finished another volume of poetry and was halfway through a novel. The novel was *A Modern Lover*. The volume of poetry, titled *Pagan Poems*, was somewhat milder in its assaults on convention than its predecessor, was therefore pretty well ignored by the critics, and earned for its author the memorable epithet "Pagan" Moore. Of the twenty-six poems in the collection, five are repeated from *Flowers of Passion*, while another poem has been resuscitated from an earlier existence in *The Spectator*, hinting that overabundance was not Moore's problem at this time. At all times Moore had an almost Platonic attitude to any subject, which could be provided with a dozen appearances in lyrical, dramatic, or fictional form, then recast and combined into another work and adorned with a thousand revisions, finally becoming an anecdote or memoir. The chronological relationship between this book and *A Modern Lover* suggests possibilities of common conception between the novel and particular poems, and these will be investigated; but already Moore had arrived at ideas he was to use for the rest of his life.

Like *Flowers of Passion*. *Pagan Poems* begins with a dedicatory sonnet again offered to a woman no longer actively in love, this time to "I d'A." Not only is love now painful because unfulfilled, but it seems to be also painful in its nature; the speaker complains of "des jours dont les richesses/ M'ont brisé . . ." (days whose riches have crushed me) Much more is made in this book of the role of memory as that which gives coherence to existence, solaces pain, and embalms changing life into a changeless death in art. The "lits clairs et noirs sarcophages" (white beds and black tombs) of the last line of the poem are the white pages and black type which provide the place of last repose for an unhappy love. In step with the growing emphasis on memory is a correlative interest in events not as they might shock the presumed reader but as they are reflected in the comprehensive consciousness of the narrator, who becomes more engrossed in making discoveries about himself than in examining a more or less debased environment.

The short and frankly undistinguished "Sonnet: Spleen" operates on a Coleridgean distinction between the poverty of the inner life and the possible riches of experience. Bemoaning the stagnation of his own life, the speaker asks for a little sin to cheer his cold heart; and thus makes it plain that the essential consideration for him is not the values of the "objective" world but the intensity of personal existence. In view of the force of this insight it is significant that the girl in "Ode to a Beggar Girl" is described as "pale and passionless." She is of interest precisely insofar as she represents a possible, and an unsatisfactory, form of experience for the poet: she is fascinating because she has become mentalized; she is not only a class object but an alternate self. Already, in writing of this girl, Moore begins to show the peculiar dualism he always betrays in writing of the poor, combining sympathetic sharing with supercilious "broad views": the almost reverential "You are very wonderful" is soon amended to "You are nothing more than a dirty beggar." The Irish landlord is apt to break at any moment into his idealized meditations about human nature and remind the peasantry of their muddy condition.

In a strange anecdote recounting a recent storm and the need to shelter from the rain in the Morgue, the poet looks at the usual accumulation of photographs, rows of stretchers, new arrivals. His ambiguous comment, "just a look sufficed," unites the same poles as those considered in his remarks on the girl, since it describes his feelings toward his own death as well as his very real disinterest in other people. It is certain that the girl is for the poet outwardly very different from himself:

> What are you? a beggar born to nothing
> Save a large inheritance of woe,
> Whilst a dilettanti poet I
> Gratify the febrile whim
> Born of pampered flesh and intellect.[1]

The "dilettanti poet," whose own large inheritance is not of woe but of twelve thousand acres of arable land and a baronial house in Mayo, is aware of himself not only as belonging to another class but also to another sphere of consciousness from the girl for whom either form of pleasure is to remain an unread book. Moore was not often to notice the quality of poetic foppery in himself save in his books specifically about the Irish social situation, *Parnell and his Island* and *A Drama in Muslin*, wherein there is the same complexity of tensions induced by the alternation between the objective and subjective views about rich and poor: in these cases he is forced to reverse a familiar process and see himself from the outside.

The point of the apparently capricious tale about the Morgue is that it was here the poet first met the beggar girl, who had come to visit a dead friend, and it was upon this occasion that the reflections upon the beggar's life began. His conclusions, taken from the outside, have a callous ring: "Death is always kindly—die:" Moore's reading of Schopenhauer, again evident in his pious wish that the girl might have a happier life in some fortunate reincarnation, does not really mitigate the case; for no philosophic warrant exists for urging suicide upon *other* people. It is not fully just to judge this statement from the outside alone, however, because the poet regards the girl as a possible condition of self, a projection for whom Schopenhauer's anodyne would be only too appropriate. In this connection one should note the frequency of references to mortality, the dead, and fatal sickness in this and other poems. Death seems to be the filter through which life is perceived; and though the conjecture must remain unproven, it may fairly be asked whether some emotional coloring like a clinical depression does not control the poetry far more strongly than purely literary tropes inherited from Baudelaire and others.

A consequence of the shift from the lyrical format in *Flowers of Passion* to the introspective, self-aware poetry of *Pagan Poems* is the growth of the narrative element. This is true because now there is a full-fledged narrator interested in his adventures for what they reveal about himself; thus every poem consists of the interplay between two kinds of fictional entity—the set of events, and the man who experiences them, and who is in a certain sense created by them. Poems like "Sonnet: Used Up" actually present two opposing views of experience as the two halves of life which the narrator must put together in the poem, which becomes the vehicle for a comprehensive and corrected vision in a more complete consciousness of the matter. In this case the complete consciousness of the matter is the result of a dialectical interplay between a profligate existence and the allures of a more settled existence in a Richmond villa. Not a very interesting or subtle interplay, one might think; yet it is the germ of many Moore novels (*Spring Days, The Lake,* perhaps *Esther Waters*), which focus upon an eminently stable and seemingly unchangeable society at the exact moment when it is penetrated by bohemian or agitating forces.

In view of the growth of this narrative element, it is not surprising that critics have found in *Pagan Poems* complete scenarios for future works of fiction. The distinguished scholar Edwin Gilcher, for example, has noticed that "La Maitresse Maternelle" contains the plot of the three-volume novel *A Modern Lover* in a verse play of less than twenty pages.[2] Albert de Crémont, a penniless artist, is discovered by the Comtesse de Beausac whose love ensures not only personal security but professional success for Albert. Crémont does love the Comtesse at first, but abandons her for a rival named Blanche; personal weakness does not allow him to break the tie, however. Inevitably he is caught out by the Comtesse and responds with the suggestion that they escape their trouble and pain by dying together. The Comtesse de Beausac may be a maternal mistress, but she is not altogether so unsophisticated in her love as that; she dismisses Albert with the complaint "Alas! a modern lover never ends so perfectly." Moore was to continue his investigation of the thesis that the nineteenth century provided an inhospitable climate for the traditional, passionate lover in *A Modern Lover* and *Mike Fletcher*. In each case the fault is to be found in the age: it is the modernity, not love, that is called into question. The peculiar sense attached to the word "modern" in Moore's writings of this period is to be found also in "A Modern Poem," where the word suggests a time of uncertainty, of messy, compromising decisions, a time qualitatively different from the past where "all is placid and still." Recalling that, after all, Jean-Jacques Rousseau had a very similar notion about retrospection, the reader might not seize what is significant here—that Moore is writing specifically of his own time, and that this writer, famous in his own day for appropriating whatever is of the latest currency, is at heart a dubiously loyal partisan of his moment in history.

Malcolm Brown is surely correct in asserting that "A Parisian Idyll," a poem about a week of love proposed for Fontainebleau, is the first version of a story, "Lovers of Orelay," published twenty-five years later in *Memoirs of My Dead Life* and offered there as autobiography.[3] Such works as *Confessions of a Young Man* and *Hail and Farewell* show Moore at work converting autobiography into fiction; but here is an amusing case of the reverse process. Perhaps the distinction is not so important. Nevertheless, *Pagan Poems* does contain an interesting mixture of facts about to become fiction, fiction about to be claimed as fact, poems about to become stories, even one novel become a poem. This poem is "Sonnet" (no subtitle), which is apparently based on Nana, the alluring heroine of Zola's novel, here as sensuous and fascinating as one might expect, but with no hinted connection with the poet. Indeed it is notable that in *Pagan Poems* a truly happy relationship with women exists only in the future. Even omitting the possibly unrepresentative "Hermaphrodite" poem and the corresponding "Sappho" with its Racinian equation of love with agony, it does seem that a number of these love poems are exercises in wish fulfillment, the product of a life in which devout wishes have not been consummated. " Joyous Death" is a poem depicting the deathbed of the poet surrounded by all his past lovers, who then serve as his pallbearers to the grave. This vicarious enjoyment of a scene at which the speaker cannot be present suggests that he is happiest with situations when he has entirely mentalized them, has displaced inwardly into the mind what might be unmanageable in the world of public events.

II A Modern Lover

While preparing *Pagan Poems* for publication, Moore was at work on his first novel. *A Modern Lover* is not only the first of his novels, it is one of his longest: a generous three volumes filled with innumerable incidents—threatened suicides, disappearing characters, many houses, balls, and a tennis match. As an elderly man of letters Moore claimed that the inclusive novelist Tolstoy must often have had a nightmare in which his latest swollen tome had unaccountably omitted a yacht race or a High Mass; but Moore began his own career with a capacious mid-Victorian novel. In scope and complexity of plot *A Modern Lover* bears a clearer relationship to an opera than to the finely balanced simplicity of his later work. An ambitious novel in terms of its depiction of large areas of the contemporary art scene, and filled with occasional touches of delicacy, the effort remains recognizably inadequate, a potboiler. That Moore himself regarded this first fictional offspring partly in the same light may be judged from the fact that he offered his novel to Tinsley, the publisher of *Lady Audley's Secret* and other early works of that formidable best-selling author, Mrs. Braddon. In any event, what Moore produced was formally a nineteenth-century "triple-decker" novel published in the expensive three-volume edition to appeal to the lucrative circulating library trade (its price of thirty-one shillings and sixpence would have made other sales difficult). Still, the amiable adulteries and unamiable condition of character of the principal figure were not calculated to please the virtuous readership of the libraries, and *A Modern Lover* was banned by both of the major circulating libraries. Moore spent a great deal of time and caustic phrasing in his subsequent battle with the censors; but, curiously, he retained a fondness for the multivolume form until the end of his career, using it overtly in *Hail and Farewell* and *Héloise and Abelard* and less plainly in the sequence novels *Evelyn Innes-Sister Teresa* and *Spring Days-Mike Fletcher-Vain Fortune.*

Moore wrote many novels about artists, but his emphasis was normally upon the psychology and moral disposition of the artist. *A Modern Lover* is specifically about the art scene in the 1870s and 1880s, and many of even the most minor figures are identifiably real members of various groups of painters, dealers, or reviewers. The dealer Mr. Bendish, who amasses enormous quantities of paintings from "The Moderns" while having apparently little idea of their true worth, seems to bear a clear relationship to Durand-Ruel, the famous art dealer who specialized in the paintings of the Impressionists. Among the adherents of the "Moderns" is an only moderately talented but abundantly enthusiastic theorist named Frazer. Frazer is a composite figure, deriving partly from the hopelessly unsuccessful musician Ernest Cabaner, of whom Moore retails the same story in *Confessions of a Young Man* as here ascribed to Frazer. In the *Confessions* version, a question arising as to the artistically destructive effect of love themes in poetry, it is pointed out that even Baudelaire's best poem was a love poem. Cabaner's triumphant response is that Baudelaire was writing about a corpse, which makes the whole thing more bearable.[4] Probably also a composite figure, Thompson, the leader of the "Moderns," partly suggests Degas in his opinions, brusqueness, and tendency to epigram. Even the central figure, Lewis Seymour, is based mostly on Moore's Paris acquaintance Lewis Weldon Hawkins; although, as Janet Egleson Dunleavy shrewdly points out, there are several hints of the young George Moore himself in the portrait of the incompetent Seymour.[5] No doubt a great deal of topicality that is now lost was plain enough in 1883: was Seymour imitating Puvis de Chavannes in his enormous classical murals, or was there some more obvious domestic influence at work? The answer that he is most of all himself, the fictional Lewis Seymour, is a good one and will have to suffice pending further scholarship. But the success of Seymour at this particular time is a cultural aspect of his fictional being, and it evidently has a great deal to do with Moore's perception of the art world of his time.

Although it was not until 1891 that George Moore became the art critic of *The Speaker*, and although his reputation as a critic was not made until *Impressions and Opinions* (1891) and especially *Modern Painting* (1893) had been published, most of his ideas on art had taken their final form by the time of *A Modern Lover*. Following Honoré de Balzac, who, he claims, was the first to discover that in the nineteenth century civilization means money, Moore derides the art of the "villa" crowd, the new consumers of painting. Great art, it seems, makes poor furniture because it is too demanding for its consumers, because anything that calls attention to itself cannot fit into a prearranged decorative schema. Consequently, the art market is controlled by the esthetics of household furnishing. Here the Irish landlord does not explicitly say, but manifestly believes, that the problem is less the dominance of money in art than the question of who is spending that money. Like Carlyle in *Past and Present* he finds offensive the "cash nexus" which replaces the older standards of social stratification in the displacement of social power to a new group untrained in the use of the amenities which power can bring. This notion is a familiar one in the landscape of Victorian arguments about education and the rise of democracy: Moore did not cease to be himself when he went to Paris in the 1870s. Incontestably a large part of Moore's thinking about the technical aspects of painting and perhaps the majority of his verbal formulations derive from his experiences in France. But the social application of these theories in England in *Modern Painting* and *Impressions and Opinions* fits very well into a continuing Victorian dispute about the role of cultural values in a new society.

In all his writings about art, Moore stresses the importance of originality, a quality which relates for him more explicitly to matters of personality than to details of execution. A mass-produced artist is not an artist at all because to be an artist means to have a significantly personal gift. As a corollary of this judgment it follows that art cannot be taught as a mere collection of techniques, that in fact such institutions as the Beaux Arts or the Kensington School of Art are actively destructive of the individual insight which is the clearest mark of talent. While controversial, these ideas are scarcely novel. But for Moore they become the basis for a denunciation of the nineteenth-century world, which has invented or brought to new perfection a number of forces harmful to art, forces which have seized control of the artist and his productions. In the first place, and preeminently, there is the belief that man in a mass democracy is systematically robbed not only of his sense of his own proper existence separate and apart from others, but he is deprived of a perception of the peculiarity of his native surroundings, made to speak a rootless, standardized form of the language in school, trained to accept standardized thinking, and induced to prefer whatever has popular approval to his own perceptions. The idea that cosmopolitanism is repugnant to true art (an idea Moore probably acquired from Degas) is systematically used to chastise the majority of artists, beginning with James McNeill Whistler, and to praise the stubborn minority including Edouard Manet and The New English Art Club who pursue their own vision. For Moore, the battle is already lost when the writer or painter operates on terms dictated by the demands of his market. Hence he is scathing in his denunciations of the modern patron, the alderman, who selects and criticizes art by committee, and of the other patron, the cleric who controls religious art, the most profitable branch of painting, using values that have no relationship at all to esthetic excellence.

Put in a certain way, all this amounts to no more than the commonplace observation that in the nineteenth century the artist is necessarily an outsider. But for Moore this alienation is a social, not a personal, fact: "The fate of all great artists in the nineteenth century is a score years of neglect and obloquy. They may hardly hope for recognition before they are fifty . . ."[6] What this means in practice is that the artist is held captive by a public taste quite different from, and necessarily inferior to, his own; a taste catered to by dealers who care nothing about art except the prices it will fetch, and by newspaper critics who write about work that is already popular and therefore trivial. In an article titled "The Failure of the Nineteenth Century," first written for *The Speaker* and subsequently collected in *Modern Painting*, Moore is compelled to follow the paradox that although the nineteenth century has been given a strong place in art by its painters, considered individually, yet as an age it stands lowest in merit.[7] The painter who stands in closest relationship to his time is a bad artist, for his time is bad for art: only the publicly unsuccessful may enter through the narrow gate which means personal greatness. For proof, Moore had only to cite in his criticism the work of scores of artists beginning with Manet; but his closest analysis of the perilous relationship between the painter and his world is to be found in *A Modern Lover*.

Before venturing on a detailed reading of *A Modern Lover*, it is worth taking a look at a remarkably apposite piece of criticism. "Sex in Art," another culling from the columns of *The Speaker* included in *Modern Painting*, deals with the complicated relationship between women and art, and with the perhaps still more complicated relationship between women and artists.[8] Moore's premise is the unfortunate sentiment that women in life are most successful in the home and in the boudoir. Jane Austen as an artist was successful because she limited herself to these essentially feminine areas; but George Eliot, he thinks, was not successful, and for the opposite reason. Because of this natural limitation of sympathy, the highest achievements of art are denied to women, who have allegiances other than artistic allegiances at all times. But for an artist to be truly triumphant in his profession, his whole mind must be given to his art: "Notwithstanding all the novels that have been written to prove the contrary, it is certain that woman occupies but a small place in the life of an artist." Lewis Seymour, the hero of *A Modern Lover*, who achieves his celebrity in the art world through women, is clearly condemned here, and the judgment is so important to Moore that he repeats it in the same article: "The great artist and Don Juan are irreparably antagonistic; one cannot contain the other." Really it is not very surprising that Moore sought a fictional test for his ideas in *A Modern Lover* because his criticism is invariably characterological. He is less interested in the geometry or brushwork of a painting than in the sensibility of the man who produces that painting, which is nothing but the embodiment of certain fundamental traits of individual character, and which constitutes a sort of permanent and public comment on the probity of its creator.

A Modern Lover begins, not astonishingly, in the shop of an art dealer, Bendish, in an atmosphere of haggling about the value of certain paintings. Bendish, who is clearly in control of the argument, stands surrounded by his miscellaneous acquisitions—ballet girls, railway stations, and all the representatives of depraved popular taste—assembled only by the principle of shrewd calculation of future market values. His artist-client, Lewis Seymour, is described in terms which relate to his weak and lascivious nature; his "feminine grace" and "exquisite beauty" mark him as a man who will attract others for reasons other than his intrinsic skill. Soon discouraged, Lewis leaves the shop and begins to contemplate suicide.

Seeing two young men discussing a ball, Seymour thinks of a picture, "The Suicide," which has recently had a powerful effect upon him. Ignorant of his creator's often repeated and vigorous distaste for paintings that relate anecdotes, Seymour remembers with some poignancy the representation of a pair of men discussing the anticipated pleasures of the evening while the wall behind them carries a placard announcing the news of a recent suicide. The force of Seymour's response to the painting is in proportion to its special applicability to himself, for it contains both sides of his attitude to life. Originally seeking for "pleasure and fame" on his arrival in London, now he is so downcast that he is impelled to kill himself, and is indeed on the point of doing so until he thinks that his fellow lodger Gwynnie Lloyd might give him some money. Already he is thinking of a woman as a protector, a provider. But his attitude to women carries with it a further complexity; he sees the well-dressed ladies on the way home as "a vision of perfumed lace in which he would one day be laid at rest." Curiously, there is in his devotion to women an element of the death-wish because, following the peculiar logic of some of Moore's early poetry, death is an escape from the complex demands of life, is the solution for weak natures to the daily challenges of experience analogous to the protective, maternal instinct he seeks in his lovers.

Receiving the help he anticipates from Gwynnie, and thus becoming a sort of prostitute in life as he is later to be in art, Seymour is elated to find a commission waiting for him. The elation proves to be necessarily short-lived, however, when Seymour is unable to finish the commission without a model. Gwynnie agrees to pose despite her religious scruples, and makes the sacrifice: Seymour, who cannot make hard choices himself, constantly forces these dilemmas upon other people. Shortly afterwards, Gwynnie disappears, actuated by feelings of shame. Lewis pursues his career with only the mildest curiosity as to her whereabouts. He has, after all, found a new protectress.

One day Lewis is seen in Bendish's shop by Mrs. Bentham, a rich divorcée; seeing future commissions and thus future profits in Mrs. Bentham's evident admiration of Lewis Seymour, Bendish introduces the pair. And they do form an interesting pair, linked as they are by their love of clothes and adornment (Moore considers this an essentially "feminine" characteristic). Lewis wants to escape life, to transcend the challenge of time, to find a person who will serve as guardian: Mrs. Bentham wants something to do; is afraid, in fact, of wasting her time; is looking for someone to look after. There is even a certain symmetry in their upbringing, for Mrs. Bentham has been raised by a devoted father, Lewis by an over-devoted mother. And Lewis brings with him a history which predisposes him to this relationship. The distinguished French critic Jean Noel has noted with some surprise that this book, coming near the beginning of Moore's friendship with Émile Zola, does not bear any obvious Naturalistic technique.[9] This is questionable. It is true that many of Zola's novels involve an investigation of a certain kind of milieu which Moore was not to attempt until A Mummer's Wife, but the explicitly theoretical aspects which underlie Zola's work have in large part to do with the exploration of family history as it bears on character. Matters of atmosphere and milieu become important only because Zola often (as does Moore) concentrates on the unstable personality unequal to the choices of life, and therefore a personality shaped by the experiences of life. In A Modern Lover family histories, and not only Seymour's, have a decisive influence on character; but the central case of Seymour is of particular interest.

Lewis Seymour is the son of a country doctor who is strongly inclined to the study of chemistry. Unfortunately Seymour's mother not only despises chemistry, she disapproves of the hours of seclusion necessary to such a pursuit, and she delivers the predictable ultimatum to the unhappy doctor. Seymour's father gives in, not without considerable suffering, and abandons his chemistry for his wife (and thus makes what is for Moore the wrong choice, pursuing the role of lover in preference to that of life's work). This act of moral cowardice weighs heavily with him, however; the remainder of his life is spent in melancholy drudgery and concluded by a generally suspected, though unproven, suicide.

A similarity to Moore's own life can be detected, for he, too, felt that his father had committed suicide (though his theory was received with irritation by others in the Moore family). Like Seymour, the novelist had an intelligence that dawned only slowly, and as Janet Egleson Dunleavy points out, many of the ideas Seymour expresses may be supposed to have been possessed by Moore as he began his abortive career as a painter.[10] A trait almost universally present in Moore's writing, but most prominently in *A Modern Lover* and *Confessions of a Young Man*, is to treat a past self as a discrete fictional character having only historical continuity with the present consciousness of the narrator—an interesting case can be made out for *Hail and Farewell* as a novel demonstrating the process by which this shedding of the past is accomplished. To be sure, this is not unlike the simple incorporation of autobiographical material into fiction that is characteristic of any writer as he casts about for a subject. But for Moore the mechanism by which this is accomplished is derived from his sense that the narrator of any work is as fictional as the events through which he must find his way. The narrative impulse observed in *Pagan Poems* is correlative to the creation of the sense of self which any experience involves. Hence the self is constantly modified by new experiences. The significance of Lewis Seymour is not only that he represents, as he undoubtedly does, an artist manqué, but also that the artist who has got lost is a past George Moore.

At just about the same time that Lewis becomes involved with Lucy Bentham, the novel begins to investigate the art movement known as "The Moderns." Like Lewis, the Moderns remain notably unpopular, neglected by the newspapers, ignored by the prosperous dealers; but, unlike him, they are not in the least downcast by this situation. The contrapuntal relationship between Lewis and the Moderns is developed in other ways, too. A theory is evolved by the novelist Harding and the painter Frazer that the contemporary art scene is crippled by sentimentality because of the influence of women: "if all modern art is based on love it is owing to them." Yet even in this sanctuary of austere artists, the taint of the time is not altogether mitigated; for Frazer is described as living on a shilling a day and making his wife live on less. His willingness to let his wife bear the greater part of the burden imposed by his vocation is a weakness of character which helps explain the fact that he is regarded as the lowest in artistic attainment among the Moderns. Frazer, perhaps, is atypical, is certainly neither a characteristic figure among the Moderns nor a dominant one. Actually, there is a sort of dual leadership in this new art movement shared by the painter Thompson, and by Harding, who, as a novelist, acts as an apologist and propagandist for the new school. Thompson is perceived generally as a manifestation of a heroic level of the expression of personality; his "iron will" contrasts sharply with the soft dependency of Seymour, and is indicative of an altogether more rigid application to his craft: "the love, the dreams, the joys and sentiments he had ruthlessly torn out of his heart and flung like flowers under the resistless wheels of the chariot of art." Harding, who considers his writing to be the equivalent of the new painting because of its insistence on contemporary history and interest in the social delineation of the age, occupies roughly the same position in the Moderns in England as that filled in France by Zola, the novelist and publicist of Manet. Since Harding, a recurrent figure in Moore's novels, is evidently a sort of representation of Moore himself (though in a somewhat more consistently cynical and sophisticated guise than Moore was able to assume), it becomes apparent that Moore's ambition to be the English Zola meant something more than the mere acquisition of a literary ideology.

Looking for a plausible reason to maintain her connection with the pleasant young Seymour, Lucy Bentham invites him to Claremont, her home is Sussex, to execute some decorative painting in the ballroom. This first great commission for Seymour is all too symptomatic: not only is the function of his work to provide incidental glitter for social occasions, but the finished paintings themselves create the effect of a "gigantic ball dress." All of Seymour's work serves, in reality, as a kind of ironic reflection of his personality. It was a painting of Venus that proved so difficult until Gwynnie agreed to be the model. Hereafter Seymour's pursuit of the love theme is insistent but not a little uncertain: his great successes in later life are to come with his Clytemnestra and his Sappho, subjects whose relationship to love is a little threatening. Of course, one of the corollaries of the very modernity of this lover is that he cannot, in fact, love. All his lady friends come to realize his worthlessness as a man and an artist, and the inability to rise above self-indulgence that is a leading feature of that worthlessness. Even on the physical level he is never disposed to find sexual fulfillment with either Gwynnie Lloyd or Mrs. Bentham; his inclinations in that area are mild. If financial success for Lewis Seymour depends upon his ability to be loved, it remains true that for him love is as mundane as business, to be used as shrewdly, to be discarded as coolly. In all

Moore's novels the test of virtue is abnegation, the refusal of mere self-interest. Gwynnie Lloyd, who makes her sacrifice uncomplainingly and bears her sufferings patiently, is already the prototype for Moore's later heroine Esther Waters, whom the novelist with only partial whimsy recalled for her goodness many times in his reminiscences. It is a hard test that Lewis Seymour fails, a hard imperative that Gwynnie and the painter Thompson face; and for an explanation of this stern code one is driven to remember that as a young man George was known as "Kant Moore" because of his interest in the German philosopher.

Still, Lucy Bentham, though pitiable, is no more capable of disinterested action than is Lewis himself. Framed by the almost superhuman dedication and virtue of Thompson and Gwynnie, the central events of the novel concern themselves with the activities of three spoiled children—Lucy, Seymour, and, later, Lady Helen. Weak and unstable, Lucy is unable to rise above her foibles and respond to the demands of life. A scruple of her own is overcome by the fact that it is at her father's suggestion that she invites Seymour to Claremont. She then reflects that fate is always leading her to do what she inwardly wishes yet dares not articulate. Lewis arouses her frustrated maternal instincts; she is unable to resist; she is in this way forced into a series of false positions—false mother, fake mistress, sham art patron. Haunted by the thought that she is wasting her time in life, she makes Seymour's career her vocation, going so far as to buy up his paintings in secret in order to increase demand on the art market. Seymour's conquest of the art establishment is mostly due to Lucy: not surprisingly, this muse of worldly success is seen playing a song from *Faust* on Seymour's first evening at Claremont (and later, in Paris, accompanies him to a performance of the same opera). But, for Moore, one loses one's soul by the simple inability to possess it. Lucy and Lewis play both roles—Faust and Mephistopheles—for each other.

During Seymour's sojourn at Claremont Mrs. Bentham is chaperoned by her friend and cousin Mrs. Thorpe, a lady offering a considerable contrast with Lucy because of her fidelity to her dead husband, her taciturnity, and her indifference to fashion. Mrs. Thorpe's ability to maintain her perseverance through long years is associated with her lucidity: it is she who is able to predict Seymour's marriage to Lady Helen. Like Thompson and unlike Lucy, she is undefeated by time, refuses to take refuge in sensations. Her prediction of the marriage to Lady Helen is based simply on her sense of the way things are, that Mrs. Bentham is aging and attached, and that Lady Helen is a fine match. Lucy and Lewis, who possess no such clear-sightedness about events, are inevitably manipulated by them. Those who are able to act decisively are they who first perceive clearly, who do not delude themselves, who are not satisfied by appearances. Seymour, lacking all of these qualifications, comes to fulfill the prophecy, not in the simple way that fate seems to indicate, but through a tawdry complexity of infidelities.

Lady Helen is described as a great beauty, one of the handsomest women of her generation. Yet at her first appearance she appeals to Seymour not for her sexual charms but for her "decorative gracefulness." More curiously still, her waist suggests "more of the Bacchus than the Venus de Milo"; again she is "beautifully decorative." Her almost sexless beauty recalls the "feminine grace" and "too developed hips" of Seymour himself. The two are, indeed, very alike: Moore argues that their immediate and mutual attraction is the impulse to self-love suggested by like natures. Unlike Lucy Bentham, Lady Helen has no maternal impulses; she is merely like Lewis Seymour but very much the stronger. A father's girl, hence spoiled, she nevertheless possesses sufficient energy to sustain Lewis in his doubtful eminence in the London art world.

A Modern Lover is a highly visual novel. An interesting exercise would be afforded by simply tracking down the pictorial sources of a number of scenes in the novel—here a Whistler river-view, here a Manet group—but it is certain that this fascination with the visual goes beyond mere allusiveness; it is a fascination occasioned by the very theme of the work. Lady Helen is described at first as almost a modulation of light: "The light filled Lady Helen's saffron-coloured hair with strange flames, and the red poppies in her straw hat echoed, in a higher key, the flowers embroidered on her dress." It is an extraordinary description. First, the passage allows the light, as it would do in a painting, to define the significant details, linking the flowers on the hat and the dress. Flowers are important here and everywhere in *A Modern Lover* (Lucy and Lady Helen are seen together in a later scene as a poppy side by side with a lily). The key to this motif is to be found in the already-quoted passage about the iron-willed Thompson crushing his loves and joys "like flowers under the resistless wheels of the chariot of art." Even in this first novel Moore has learned his great lesson from Wagner, that the use of such motifs can gain much narrative density. Secondly, the description of Lady Helen, even with its optical precision, is already deflected into musical conceptions with its invocation of a "higher key" and the "echo" of the floral pattern. Music always remained a powerful model for Moore, supplying him with a fluid sense of form in narrative rhythm and thematic development and transforming the example of Wagner into a genuinely innovative fictional device. *A Modern Lover* is one of the few cases in literature in which one can observe the process of cultural crossover by which the different arts come to interpenetrate each other to produce something new and valuable. Moore's novels in their turn were to be read by the young James Joyce, who used the device of musical structure to great effect in his novel *Ulysses* and in the more extreme form of his later work *Finnegans Wake*.

To Mrs. Thorpe the advent of Lady Helen is clearly the sign that heralds the future marriage of Lewis; to Lewis himself and to Lucy Bentham no such prospect is permitted to interfere with a relationship that they both expect to endure. There is, moreover, a sense in which Lady Helen unknowingly acts to fan the very modest flames of Lucy's affair. Forewarned and still pained by the outcome of her still undissolved marriage, and in the circumscribed society of Claremont, only too aware of the social consequences of disgracing herself, Mrs. Bentham is at first very discreet in her relationship to Lewis, always presenting him as a promising painter and a guest. But seeing Lewis walking quite innocently with Lady Helen, she abandons her role of apparent aloofness and becomes jealous. It is curious that in this milieu those who are not actively lovers may yet be actively jealous. In a novel filled with dubious lovers there are still many rivals—Lucy and Lady Helen, Lewis and Mr. Bentham, Lewis and the pompous squire Lord Senton. Love is a sort of emotional property, the parallel in fact of the artistic properties which are secured in the form of nominal reputations and furthered with great competitiveness by the various schools of painters in London. And like art again, love is debased in the novel when it comes under the control of the cash nexus, when it becomes property pure and simple, when it becomes in the full, ironic sense of the title, "modern."

Not long after his first meeting with Lady Helen, Lewis announces his intention of going off to Paris, much to the consternation of Mrs. Bentham, who nevertheless agrees to provide him with funds. At first the project works well: Lewis concentrates enough on his painting that he initially remains ignorant of the world of French society and fine restaurants until a visit by Lucy persuades him of the attractions of Paris. Then, as in his student days in London, he spends less and less time at the studio and more time (and much more money) on self-indulgence. With his considerable social charm he is able to win a place in the social world, even beginning an affair with a marquise, once again substituting tangible social rewards for harder artistic successes. And Lewis does know how to enjoy his pleasant life at the cost of ignoring longer goals, a trait Moore regards as essentially feminine: "He did not look backwards or forwards; his nature allowed him the feminine luxury of burying his face deep in the present." But when this vein of luxury leads not only to enormous expenses and neglected painting but also to an affair with a marquise, Mrs. Bentham begins to look around London for a suitable studio for Seymour; and he, obeying the tug of the purse-strings, soon follows.

Logically and artistically Lewis has exhausted his potential before this point. His training in Kensington and Paris denies him a chance to develop his highly attentuated sense of self; his paintings are therefore concoctions, his ideas echoes. Yet it is not until he returns to London that Lewis really understands his impotence as an artist. From this moment he will fix his attention on the tasks he can manage best, the manipulative social acts that promote the reputation of his work with an undiscriminating public.

Adroit as was her maneuver in luring Lewis back to England, Mrs. Bentham has come almost to the end of her time. She gives a ball in the now completely redecorated Claremont, inviting Lewis's rival Lord Senton as well as her own rival Lady Helen. Lord Senton offers little in the way of competition, but Lady Helen is overwhelmingly beautiful, immediately charming Lewis and leading him to claim he does not love Mrs. Bentham because she is old enough to be his mother. Sensing competition, Lady Helen for the first time thinks of the possibility of marriage. Mrs. Bentham is not gifted with profound penetration of human affairs, but she does understand simple English: she is standing close enough to hear the whole conversation, is understandably pained, but chooses to suffer in silence. In a gesture that contains his whole soul Lewis finally asks Lucy to help pay for the wedding to Lady Helen. Generous and pitiable, but most of all helpless, she consents.

The engagement and subsequent ceremony offer a burlesque series of parodic deformations of courtship for this clumsy Don Juan as he is brought to the altar by the headstrong Lady Helen. Lady Granderville does not see why an ambassador's daughter should marry a penniless painter. Her proposal to disinherit Lady Helen deters that lady not at all, but Lewis immediately becomes alarmed. His frantic attempts to charm the old woman into a more amiable disposition are interpreted as signs of a sensible man who values power and wealth more, at any rate, than his future wife, a man who is bound to disgrace the family less than some more foolish choice of the unpredictable heiress. Having won the necessary approval from the parents and the necessary cash from Mrs. Bentham, Lewis has to choose a best man. For someone whose list of friends is exclusively female it is a difficult decision, particularly since Lewis has, as usual, one eye open for the main road to advancement. He selects a journalist, and for one of his witnesses he chooses the President of the Royal Academy.

Just before the wedding Lady Helen engages a new maid, a pockmarked young woman named Gwynnie Lloyd, now unrecognizable as Seymour's former model. Mrs. Bentham, of course, is present at the ceremony in addition to Gwynnie Lloyd, as are other former admirers of Lewis's particular talents. So filled is the church with the sound of feminine weeping that a number of guests are outraged at the plainly discreditable proceedings.

Seymour's honeymoon, though presumably less discreditable to him as a lover, is not less unsatisfactory from an artistic point of view, for his response to Lady Helen's complaints that their companionship is being limited by his sketching is simply to stop painting altogether for a time (just as previously his periods of coldness toward Mrs. Bentham had been his most fruitful bouts of work). The lover exists in a reciprocal relationship with the artist. In London again, Lady Helen finds a tactful and considerate friend in Mrs. Bentham who undertakes to help her improve her taste; the two are joined on their expeditions to antique shops and picture dealers by Gwynnie Lloyd. So now the three former rivals in love are joined in an "artistic" purpose, the decoration of Seymour's house, and in a common pursuit, the passive happiness of Lewis Seymour. It makes no difference that Lewis deserves none of this solicitude—no one reproaches him when he is caught kissing a model. He remains the eternal child, unchanged, indeed of all his contemporaries: "Time had changed him but little; his figure was as slim, his eyes as sweet, as they were ten years earlier." (Yes, Oscar Wilde *did* read this novel written some eight years before his own *Dorian Gray*. Both novels deal with the mistake of treating life as if it were art.) Time has disfigured Gwynnie Lloyd, aged Mrs. Bentham, even matured Lady Helen enough to write a sad volume of poems on the passing away of love and the ideals of the past, but Lewis does not change.

Lady Helen is anxious to get Lewis into the Royal Academy, a project that is exceedingly difficult not because of his lack of intrinsic ability so much as the opposition of the various factions in control. Faithless in all things, Seymour had, as a young man, been a partisan of the Moderns, but had abandoned that party and its astringent demands. But since the 1874 exhibition a belated recognition of the Moderns has been growing; consequently some in the Academy look with a cold eye on Seymour's candidacy on that account. And, although, ironically, Lewis owes some of his success to the confusion in the public mind between his own work and the Medievalists, the latter school remains hostile to the classical allegories that Lewis turns out year after year. Finally, it is up to Lady Helen to act. Knowing that the election hinges upon the vote of one member, a man named Holt, she agrees to receive socially Holt's wife if Holt will support Lewis. Corrupted from his purpose by his own affections for his wife, Holt does cast the decisive vote in Seymour's favor—and acts in accord with a pattern which fits many Moore heroes. (In *The Strike at Arlingford* (1893) it is the labor leader John Reid who is deflected from his mission by his fiancée, thus prompting a journalist to remark that the family is the rock upon which socialism smashes to pieces.) Not only a child, but often a venal child with the bad boy's opportunistic innocence, Seymour begins to use his wife more and more for these distasteful occasions, even encouraging her to flirt to gain him some advantage—for a favorable review, to win over some opponent, to reconcile cooling friends. On the day of his election Lewis breaks in upon a conversation in which Gwynnie, Lady Helen, and Mrs. Bentham have discovered the sacrifices that they have all made, and hence have discovered the perennial faithlessness that is the secret of this modern lover. No one now rebukes him. The final word on Lewis Seymour has, after all, been delivered long ago by the perceptive novelist Harding: "He succeeded through women. He never had a pennyworth of talent."

Partly, one suspects, to Moore's chagrin, the author of *A Modern Lover* was not commended to the public executioner, nor did the book in any way receive the excited opposition that his poetry had done; nor did it make a profit. But while this first novel was not a commercial success, it did evoke interest and some praise in public places—one reviewer noted that the gifted new writer had evidently been saved from the excesses of Zola by his Christian faith and character as a gentleman. Enough landlord remained in George Moore that the epithet "gentleman" could not have displeased him. His "Christian faith" had evaporated long before, but in the matter of the debt to Zola the reviewer was exactly right. Moore himself wrote to his French acquaintance: "The fact that my novel has been successful may interest you; for, as I have already told you, I owe you everything. My book alas is not good."[11] The value judgment recorded here was not one confided to anyone else, so it may have been merely a rare example of professional modesty, or perhaps a less rare case of self-doubt. In any event, Moore remained sufficiently unabashed to begin work immediately on the novel that was finally titled *A Mummer's Wife*, a novel which he hoped would clearly establish him as Zola's disciple in England.

III   A Mummer's Wife

Quite apart from the intentional link through Zola and their close proximity in time, *A Modern Novel* and *A Mummer's Wife* are works with important continuities. Due to the failure of *A Modern Lover* to prosper in its triple-decker format, Moore began to look around for a publisher who would circumvent the expensive library edition market by publishing as cheaply as possible in one volume. He found his man in an aging publisher of translations named Henry Vizetelly. Vizetelly would later go to prison, and die there, for publishing translations of Zola. (At the time of his meeting with Moore, Vizetelly had not published any of Zola's work: conjecturally, at least part of Moore's often-expressed grief at Vizetelly's death was due to the part he played in encouraging the older man's enthusiasm for the French master.) Both novels deal with life-choices: if Moore can be assigned a single, dominant theme it is the question of choosing an appropriate vocation in life. In both cases the protagonist is unequal to the demands of his calling because of some fundamental weakness of character. It may be paradoxical to equate the prosperous and worldly Lewis Seymour with the often pathetic and invariably ineffectual Kate Ede; in reality all that separates them is the social class they inhabit and the fact that Kate is less able to make Seymour's shrewd equation between security and conserving to the full one's very limited abilities.

The social class difference between Kate Ede and Lewis Seymour is not a trivial barrier; at least not for George Moore, who returns to specific social analysis in all his books about Ireland, in some of his plays, and most of all in *Esther Waters*. Indeed *A Mummer's Wife* is prefaced by a quotation from Victor Duruy's *Introduction to the History of France* on the importance of one's milieu: "Change the surroundings in which man lives, and, in two or three generations you will have changed his physical constitution, his habits of life, and a goodly number of his ideas." So relevant is this quotation to the theme of the novel that it is important not to overstress or misinterpret it. There is no evidence at all in any of Moore's work that he considered environment totally decisive to the exclusion of all other influences. Rather, a common-sense rendering of this notion makes it clear that while people are, undoubtedly, affected by their milieu, they do, in a certain sense remain the same (unlike Duruy, Moore is interested in the question of changes within a single generation). The point of Kate Ede's varied career, after all, is that she is as deficient in the first half of her life as in the second, and for the same reasons.

·William James has a theory that dramatic conversions are the result of an early indoctrination with religious notions that stress the discontinuity between the sinner and the saint: not to be one simply means to become the other. Psychology, of course, knows no such discontinuities. For unstable personalities there may be nothing more than a simple oscillation, a successive acceptance of competing philosophies of life; for such people it is the vacillation itself that as truly constitutes the self as any form that external cultural forces impose upon it. Kate Ede, who makes such a choice between cultural extremes in *A Mummer's Wife*, undergoes a classical change—from churchgoer to drunkard; from seamstress to bohemian; from nurse to patient. And yet, as will be seen, in many ways she remains the same.

Growing financial difficulties force Kate to take a lodger (one of the virtues of this book is its insistence on strict physical and psychological causality, a virtue carried here almost to the heights attained only by Daniel Defoe in the English novel). Dick Lennox, the lodger, is an actor in a provincial touring company, not a very successful, nor, one suspects, a very gifted, actor; but his intrusion into the Ede household is an extraordinary event of great importance for Kate. With her limited nature she is not likely to be fascinated by the appeal of an actor as a humble servant of art. What Dick Lennox most of all represents for her is the allure of another kind of life, the glittering promise of bohemian existence, a liberation from the cheerless cell of actuality. To the unbearable regularity of Kate's existence Dick seems to bring an active principle of disorder. On his first appearance he wastes what seems to Kate an unaccountable amount of time doing nothing at all, suddenly remembers an appointment and is about to rush off when the mention of dinner causes him to forget about his appointment again. Then he pursues the question of possible dishes and methods of preparation, and finally decides that, regrettably, there might not be time to eat after all. Kate is puzzled and attracted by this scene, which awakens in her all her dormant emotionalism. Her subsequent reactions to Lennox have a certain duality about them: recalling a conversation with him, she remembers his kindness and not his rudeness; walking through town, she imagines him walking after her, yet protests violently when he does make advances.

Sharply imagined as she is, still Kate Ede is a provincial type. Dick Lennox, who has played a role or two (he specializes in depicting the "bad man" who seduces married women in his plays), recognizes the type and proceeds to cast Kate Ede into his own drama. Neither of the principal actors in this pottery-town interlude is quite suited to his part. Lennox is fat, not very young, jolly rather than impressive. Kate lacks the lucidity to understand her role at all, and for the opening scenes wavers between the disapproving matron and the passionate heroine. Inevitably there develops an unmistakable strain of low comedy as the infelicitous lovers contrive to stumble through their unsubtle movements of seduction and courtship (and lend to their creator a peculiarly ungallant appearance of contempt for his characters: his alienation from the lives of his characters foreshadows the famous indifference shown by Joyce in *Dubliners* and *A Portrait of the Artist as a Young Man*). In the most memorable incident Dick accompanies Kate on a tour of a local factory, finally succeeding in stealing an embrace in a room filled with tea services and other ceramic objects of even greater utility. Love among the chamber pots is the subject for farce; there follow all the little events of a farce—the meetings on the stairs, the whispered conversations always interrupted, the untidy elopement. Finally, Kate does run away with Dick Lennox, almost missing the train and in great fear lest she be recognized before she can make good her escape.

Until this point Kate has been marked by a remarkable passiveness. Scarcely acquiescent in her attitude to her life in Hanley, she yet has not struggled against it or taken a single step that would liberate her inner desires. Dick Lennox actively interposes into this existence; had he not appeared, Kate would no doubt have lived and died in the same house, the same occupation, the same gray routine (all of Moore's failed characters fall short of effective being because of a certain lack of energy). But now comes the turning point of her life; given the chance to assert herself, she has to fall back upon the doubtful vitality of an uncultivated fund of sentiment which has never been able to take the cool measure of reality. It is important to realize that *A Mummer's Wife* is not a sort of Gray's "Elegy" lamenting the loss of genuine powers in an uncongenial setting; Moore tellingly lists the characteristics of Kate Ede that are now given free rein—"febrile," "hysterical," "intoxicated."

Intoxication, in fact, becomes the controlling metaphor for Kate's life. Describing her as the child left at home by her pious mother, Moore has this to say of the idle stories she hears from the lady who looks after her during the day: "The little girl considered these hours quite delicious, and her childish brain was thus early *intoxicated with sentiment.*" (Italics mine) The bohemian existence into which sentimentality thrusts her does cause her to drink almost immediately in order to put away the residual inhibitions of her life in Hanley. Urged by Dick to "put a little gaiety into the part," she takes a few glasses of sherry, skipping from the grim realities of her previous life to the undemanding scenes of childhood. There is a strict equivalence for Kate Ede between sentimentality and insobriety. She drinks not only, as the classical drunkard, to forget, but also to be: her drinking is constitutive in that it allows her to reach the alienated world from which she has been debarred by the limitations of an unsatisfying experience. But merely to state the equation is to recognize its inadequacy. For Kate this indulging in sentiment becomes a destructive act because of the violence with which reality is thrust aside and forced to yield its place to formless and undisciplined emotions. In Hanley she had in many ways been a model wife, bearing with the tedious litany of complaints that her invalid husband uttered by the hour, and putting up with a querulous mother-in-law with exemplary patience. After her elopement and subsequent marriage to Dick Lennox these qualities disappear as soon as she abandons the mass of social tissues that nurture them: to Dick's astonishment the kind, blond woman he knew at Hanley becomes a shrewish, jealous, insatiable wife with an inexplicable compulsion to drink.

Some of Dick's perplexity arises from an ironic miscalculation: his sojourn at the Ede household has made him aware of domestic security and converted him to a yearning for a settled way of life with this young woman as companion. He does not comprehend that for Kate to be an actor's wife means to be free once and for all of such regulated tedium; for her the difference between the bourgeois and the bohemian is primarily a psychological one, a difference not easily to be reconciled or obliterated. Her behavior as an imperfect and termagant wife is consistent with the disruptive and un-methodical relationships she sees around her—the casual affairs between actors and actresses, the subtle but nontheless certain lesbian affair between Dolly and Beaumont, the theatrical fiction that compels her to call herself *Miss* Kate D'Arcy. A stable marriage founded on such a profound collision of purposes is evidently not to be hoped for. Yet at first the completeness of the reversal makes a workable arrangement, for it is Dick who becomes the kind and considerate spouse to Kate's increasingly difficult nature; and their marriage offers a clear negative image of Kate's previous marriage to Ralph Ede.

There is a true turning point to be observed in Kate's flight with Dick Lennox. Her marriage marks the beginning of the decline of the material fortunes of the touring company, which even with the modest expectations of a circuit which takes in Hanley, Leeds, Wigan, Huddersfield, and Rochdale, is faced with such imminent straits that the owners decide to break up the tour. Kate begins to drink more and more, becomes more and more jealous, as she sees her new life threatened by exactly the same pressures that made existence in Hanley so unendurable. Distressed at first, then alarmed, Dick goes through the bewildered reactions occasioned by his frequently unreasonable and sometimes actually violent wife. At one point he tries committing her for a time to an asylum, sitting by her on the cart "huge, kind, and indifferent, even as the world

itself." His demeanor at this moment is striking, partly for its reflection of the ethical universe that is the home of all these men and
women, but more importantly because his attitude to Kate—kindness as well as indifference—has precisely reduplicated Kate's own
rather abstracted concern for Ralph Ede's illness in the opening
pages of the novel.

The moral symmetry of the characters in *A Mummer's Wife* as
they circle around in repeated movements produces a sort of narrative logic which begins to control the sequence of incidents and
gives the sense of inevitable detail which so distinguishes the work.
If Kate grows to resemble Ralph and Dick to resemble the Kate of
her earlier life, it is only necessary to recall the instability of that
first union to realize that there will be another abandonment, that
Dick will finally leave Kate, just as she abandoned Ralph Ede so
long ago. Promising a reconciliation if Kate ceases drinking, an injunction tantamount to wishing Kate to cease to be herself, Dick
promises financial support, but insists upon a separation.

And there are still other derisory complexities to be remarked in
this rhythmic dance before it is done. Brillat Savarin's famous dictum that one could tell what a man is from what he eats could here
be amended to the rule that one can tell what a man is from whom
he marries. One day Kate happens to meet Ralph Ede on the street.
Both evince curiosity at each other's life, both have much to tell, but
it is Ralph who makes the most illuminating revelation. He, too, has
remarried, this time to Kate's former assistant Miss Hender. But
marriage to the aggressive Miss Hender (whom Kate had considered
too worldly) has changed the complaining and dilatory husband into
quite a different man. His cough indeed remains; yet now it is he
who has to listen to repeated grumbling, who has to hurry his steps
lest he occasion suspicion by remaining out too long: "If Mrs. Ede
heard of the meeting she would kick up an awful row. She would hit
him, knock him all over the place, which was very cruel of her. . . ."
Having lost Kate, Ralph marries a woman who acts to him just as the
later Kate does to Dick Lennox. Following this final insight, Kate's
death is almost anticlimactic; such is the economy of the action in
this novel that only four calendar years have elapsed since her de-
sertion of Ralph Ede.

If a criticism can be applied to *A Mummer's Wife* it is that its
constriction of vision produces a certain lack of imaginative variety.
Nevertheless, it is certain that Moore nowhere else demonstrates

such concentrated control over his plotting: there have been those critics who see this work as his very best. *A Mummer's Wife* was the first of Moore's books (and one of the last) to sell well, running through twenty editions in eight years in England, and through two pirated editions in America in the same period. Critical reaction at the time was divided into three groups. The first, predictably, was put off by the too-uncompromising realism of the narrative, and saw the sinister menace of Zola in the general conception: *The Academy* dismissed the plot as "repulsive." A few were pleased by the novel as an artistic success, these being almost without exception critics already disposed to look favorably upon the new Naturalistic tendencies of European literature. A third group was frankly incredulous that George Moore, a man known chiefly for not very cogently expressed opinions at social gatherings, could produce anything approaching a work of art. George Bernard Shaw thought the idea was nonsense. (Shaw's unreceptive attitude was not unique for him. Years later he refused to subscribe to the first edition of James Joyce's *Ulysses*, saying no Irishman could be expected to pay such a price for a book.)

CHAPTER 3

Ambitions and Experiments

I A Drama in Muslin

A Mummer's Wife is generally considered Moore's most Naturalistic work, even though the influence of Gustave Flaubert is at least as important as that of Zola. Certainly it is the last of Moore's writings to permit of such easy classification, for from this point on he is both more catholic in his borrowings and more capable in his determination to fix his own stamp on his work, whatever the source. In 1885 appeared a book that was to influence the novelist for the rest of his life, *Marius the Epicurean* by Walter Pater. Even by generous standards, Pater's novel is not very impressive as finished narrative, but it does have in every line what Moore possessed then only occasionally—finished style. *Marius* is first of all an imaginative reconstruction of the experience of living in a vanished culture, the late Roman Empire: this task Moore was to undertake in *Héloise and Abelard*, *The Brook Kerith*, and many other of his later works.

In its hero Pater's novel offers a type who is to become central for Moore's subsequent work, the self-conscious young man, last of his race, who concerns himself with the problem of how to maintain the undoubted values of the past in the face of problematic contemporary innovations. When *Marius* first appeared Moore had already been at work for some time on *A Drama in Muslin*; hence his excitement can in part be explained by the similarity in theme between Pater's work and his own. *A Drama in Muslin* springs from Moore's intuitive (and historically shrewd) persuasion that the great days of the Irish aristocracy were irrevocably ended. Alice Barton is no Marius, but she does face choices clearly analogous to those of the young pagan (like his, her faith tends to the agnostic). All the affinities that Moore detected between himself and the young

52

Marius are to be found in Alice, who observes the decay of a civilization no longer vital enough to sustain itself; she perceives the inefficacy of Catholicism (like Moore) as Marius did the shortcomings of the older religion of Numa. Like Moore and Marius, Alice substitutes for the outmoded allegiances of religion a commitment to experience that is almost devout in its ethical intensity. Like Moore (but in this unlike Marius), she chooses finally to seek this experience outside her native land.

Drama must have been much on Moore's mind as he wrote this novel. Not only had he just completed a novel *(A Mummer's Wife)* about an actress who lacks discrimination to separate the worlds of fantasy and fact, but he was also the author of a disastrous tragedy, *Martin Luther*, and the recent translator of *Les Cloches de Corneville*, the play that marks Kate Ede's theatrical debut. Consequently, the drama is a constant metaphor in the novel, with its frequent references to dressing up, playing roles—and an actual performance at the outset of the action of "King Cophetua and the Beggar Maid," a piece of dramaturgy composed by Alice Barton, one of the main characters in the novel. This imagery extends to comparatively minor details. There are several passages in the novel where segments from different conversations are reported at the same time in alternating speeches. Critics have seized upon these passages as evidence of the influence of Flaubert, who uses a similar method in the "comices agricoles" section of *Madame Bovary*. Moore's knowledge and general esteem of Flaubert is undisputed, but the technique is a common one in drama, and its use here is probably due rather to the prevailing analogy in the novel than to any debt to Flaubert. At all events the use of a central image is not unique for Moore, who often used this structural effect to advantage, employing the metaphor of intoxication in *A Mummer's Wife*, of gambling in *Esther Waters*, and so on.

The novel opens with the graduation ceremony of five Irish girls from a convent school. In a sense it is their drama: Moore in the preface indicates that the men in the novel are mere "silhouettes" to serve as a kind of decorative background to this study of women in contemporary Ireland. Like the peasantry of the 1880s, women are coming, in a confused way, to see their anomalous position in society: necessary, but inferior. All five are soon to be presented at the Viceregal Court in Dublin to mark their entry into what, from time immemorial, has been called the "marriage market," where women either become eligible commodities or resign themselves to a long spinsterhood. It is a time of change (many of Moore's novels concern themselves with the uneasy adjustments of cultural transformation), and in the group of five may be observed the diverse attitudes possible to such changes. Two of the girls, Olive Barton and Violet Scully, are open adherents of the traditional view voiced by Mrs. Barton that "a woman is absolutely nothing without a husband"; the subsequent competition for the hand of Lord Kilcarney is to become an exclusive contest between them. Another pair, composed of Cecelia Cullen and May Gould, is hostile to the respectable, accepted opinion, causing the two to react violently against received standards; May becomes frankly promiscuous, while Cecelia grows antisocial, bitter, and clearly lesbian. Between these two polarities Alice Barton is forced to find her way. In a milieu characterized by radical discontinuities and misproportion on both personal and social levels she is an integrative figure, trying to construct a viable point of view that will bind together the confusion around her.

The point of the dramatic analogy is that it so plainly delineates the opposition between what is real and what is merely supposed to be real in a limited and hypothetical situation. For the peasants in the snow, gazing like spectators at a play into the windows of a ball in Galway, the luminous events they witness contrast like some fanciful comedy with the intractable facts of their own existence. Either there are two distinct realities, poverty paralleling but never meeting its twin world of frivolity, or one is a mere sham performance, concealing only for a moment the devastating facts of starvation and cold. Alice Barton alone among the characters is lucid enough to wish for a bridge between the way things are and the glittering mask which disguises them. She has already begun "to see something wrong in each big house being surrounded by a hundred small ones, all working to keep it in sloth and luxury." This perception is a remarkable one for an Irish landlord of the period to put into the mouth of a character in his novel, no matter how long his residence in Paris; in *A Drama in Muslin* Moore is as aware of both compartments of experience as Alice Barton (though he is not constantly so level-headed. Critics have complained about the schizophrenia of his other writings on Ireland).

Alice Barton herself writes a drama, "King Cophetua and the Beggar Maid," which revolves between two kinds of reality, commitment to the ordinary world of marriage and procreation and the other, ideal world of poetry and music. Like Alice, King Cophetua undergoes searching choices before he finally decides upon marriage. Seeing her play in performance Alice is repelled because of the transformation which interposes between the ideal conception and the actual reenactment by living human beings: "The idea as it passed into reality had become polluted." A source of this revulsion, as will be seen, is Alice's difficulty in accepting the sexual interpretation that most actors would make of Cophetua's final choice for the lady. Shortly thereafter Alice reacts in a similar way when she sees a tableau-vivant of the Christmas manger scene acted at the convent school. Only to Alice Barton is the representation absurd and gauche, for she is unwilling to concede that this universal symbol of domesticity can have any link with divinity. By her clear, cold mind inherited from her mother Alice has a strong sense of the actual: but her dreamy, ineffectual, and frequently scatterbrained father has endowed her with a keenly felt yet unearthly idealism. There is consequently in her disposition a need to reunite the real and the ideal, to both of which her bifurcated consciousness responds on different levels. Her often-expressed opinion is that the best kind of life consists in making both ends meet, in making the ends of nature the ends of personal aspiration; but to state a solution is not to arrive at it: Alice's adjustment to the ends of nature is a deliberate and intricate one.

In *Defensio pro Scriptis Meis* (1887) Moore is to recall Alice Barton's situation in these words: "Higher than Alice no woman could go; any higher advance must be attended by unwillingness to accept the double duties of life." What is implied by this opaque comment is simply that Alice's idealism sometimes inclines her to be a prude. Whenever a scene is reduced to human relationships drawn on the plainest physical level, Alice takes fright, whether over what she conceives of as a misinterpretation of her own play or the manifest sexual involvement between May Gould and Fred Scully—the latter an arrangement which elicits from Alice undisguised shock. This ascetic quality in Alice's personality occasionally deceives her into a misconstruction of quite evident realities, as is the case with her failure to penetrate the complex hanky-panky between her mother and Lord Dungory. Moore, however, seems determined to underline the permanently animalistic and primitive qualities which are present behind respectable facades in this most sexually conservative of countries. He is not deceived by the apparently innocuous

ceremony by which girls are received at Court, preferring to see in
the traditional kiss of the Lord Lieutenant a lingering survival of the
custom by which the virginity of a maiden is sacrificed to her feudal
lord on the first night of her marriage. And in a derisory comment
on the Dublin gossips who are quick to retail each new scandal, he
compares one such old lady to a female hound, "her nose in the air,
her capstrings hanging lugubriously on either side of her weather-
beaten cheeks," baying aloud the news to her canine cohorts.

The layer of intractable fact that is hidden by social convention is
not totally concealed from Alice. As a feminist she is aware that
women, in their own way, are as oppressed as the peasantry and that
society's insistence on the appearance of purity and virtue in women
actually inhibits the acquisition of true virtues and thus promotes
their opposites. But once again the "double duties of life" require
that the search for equality does not mean a wholesale rejection of
unavoidable truths about human relationships. Moore is adamant
that only foolishness or perversity can lead one to forget the "im-
mutable laws of life" and condemn sexual love because of an over-
emphasis on the necessary struggle for freedom. Alice, who does in
the end marry and find a satisfactory relationship with Edward
Reed, is at length willing to settle for relative equality within limits.
To their domestic economy he is to bring three hundred pounds a
year from his practice, she, two hundred from her writing.

While Alice does come in time to recognize the laws of life, her
friend Cecelia Cullen is unable to act with the same proportion,
indeed she carries her reaction against woman's lot to the point of
hatred and revolt. In this other feminist there is a sort of temptation
for Alice, who sees many of her own ideas carried further and
reflected back as challenges to her own position. Alice begins her
search for unity from the bleak perception that life is radically
dichotomized, but Cecelia tells her plainly that "the real and the
ideal are not one but twain." Again, it is Alice's idealism that at first
makes it difficult to come to terms with aggressive male sexuality;
but Cecelia's idealism leads her to reject masculine love entirely. In
a lesbian declaration of tenderness, Cecelia tells Alice that they are
betrothed in eternity, her own intense religious feelings coloring
the choice of words in a way that is not possible for Alice, whose
aversion to Catholicism springs from a conviction that it is "human
even unto bastardy." Having eternity ahead of her, Cecelia is to
retire finally to a convent to await her soul-mate. Just as Alice is at

first perplexed by the deformities which the participation of live actors seem to impose on her plays, Cecelia is also prone to find in art a bastion against reality. Unable to secure a satisfactory footing in an uncongenial world, she shuts herself up and plays Bach. (This curious equation is found again in Arthur Barton, who is sufficiently preoccupied by his painting to ignore with apparent equability his wife's flirtation with Lord Dungory. The fleeting presence of the cynical and actively heterosexual novelist John Harding in the narrative gives assurance that a particular danger, rather than a general truth about art and sexuality, is being expounded here.)

Cecelia's disappearance into the convent removes her in the clearest possible way from the marriage market, prompting the shallow but not inapposite comment from Olive that "it is by far the best thing she could do, for she couldn't hope to be married." From a quite different point of view Alice has concluded earlier in the novel that if God exists only priests and nuns can be in the right; this opinion, when related to that of Olive just given, and that of Mrs. Barton that religion is all that is respectable, forms an intuition of the interdependent roles in Ireland of religion, class, and marriage. Marriage is the institution by which the inequities of society are preserved in this world, inequities in which it fully shares. All protest against the order of society or the conventions of marriage is referred to the way things are, that is to say, definitively ignored in a fashion that makes dissenters seem wicked or revolutionary. Alice notes the injustices, but she does marry. The two "bad girls," May Gould and Cecelia Cullen, rebel against matrimonial autocracy and are banished for their pains, one to increasing profligacy, the other to a convent.

Of the five graduating Galway maidens, this reckoning accounts for three, leaving only Violet Scully and Alice's sister Olive. Alice is in many ways the mirror-opposite of her sister, a beauty whose inheritance of the full weight of her father's weak and foolish nature has made her a confident and determined competitor in the frivolous sweepstakes of Dublin courtship. She is attentive to dress, is, in fact, described meticulously and repeatedly in terms of the clothing she wears as if she were nothing but a spiritless but faultlessly robed automaton, while Alice, on the other hand, is given to dark soliloquies about the symbolism of the superficial adornment that society leads women to adopt. Mrs. Barton, who knows a clotheshorse when she sees one, expects a triumph in the form of a great

match in the Dublin season for Olive; of Alice's chances she is much
more dubious. But in this judgment Mrs. Barton is mistaken, for not
only does Alice find a husband, but Olive, despite a brilliant beginning, fails, ruining her chances with Lord Kilcarney through a dal-
liance with a young officer. In the final analysis Olive is defeated in
her hopes by her too-credulous acceptance of the external for-
malities of the muslin world, because she fails to see through the
romantic mummery to the simple, brutal facts beneath, which so
fascinate her sister. Ineffective as ever, she loses even her soldier to
the "bad woman," Mrs. Lawler, who triumphs with the unthinkable
proposition, "the same blood runs in our veins."

Alice Barton is the single individual in the novel capable of
grasping exactly the implications of having the same kind of red
blood cells as a fallen woman; but for her the process of acquiring
this evenness of vision is a lengthy one, and not without its atten-
dant paradoxes. As a feminist she marries; as a Nationalist she abandons her country and goes to live in England. James Joyce made his
Stephen Dedalus in *A Portrait of the Artist as a Young Man* assert
that the shortest way to Tara was by way of Holyhead, a claim which
depends for its force on the realization that for Stephen Dedalus, at
any rate, the assertion is consistent. Equally for Alice Barton in
Moore's much earlier novel is it true that her final choices accord
perfectly with her initial beliefs. Her Nationalism is really nothing
but her reaction to the manifest social inequities, which in Ireland,
mean that a non-working landlord class lives well at the expense of
countless sweating tenants; it is a reaction to a strictly localized
scene which she can abandon at the same time that she abandons
the locality. Her feminism is of the same order, a search for reality
in human relationships unhindered by arbitrary traditions. Neither
one allegiance nor the other is at root altered by her ultimate decisions, perhaps because they are not, in the usual sense, allegiances,
obligations owed to external beings. Moore's heroes and heroines
are most successful when they achieve the fullest measure of freedom conformable to a realistic appreciation of things, when they
most fully develop themselves as individuals or as artists.

If this psychologizing seems unsatisfactory as an approach to what
are, after all, complex social problems, still it must be considered
that the approach was the one utilized by Moore in all such discussions. For him the concrete particular is infinitely more valuable
than the abstract: Moore loves to convert large issues of theoretical

behavior into private explorations of conscience. Again and again he tests his characters by their willingness to stand up against the accepted canons of public morality, whether these involve the prejudices of the Irish landowning class, the Catholic Church, English prudery, or unexamined social inertia. Possibly such a concern with the welfare of the single consciousness is the reason for Moore's preoccupation with the subject of exile in all his writings, for exile is the event which, most of all, throws back intellectual energies onto the contemplation of self as distinct from all threatening classes or movements.

II   Confessions of a Young Man

Confessions of a Young Man (1888) is preeminently the novel in which Moore examines the emergence of self. On the first page of the novel he attempts to give some account of the origin of this process. So crucial, so often quoted, and so variously interpreted is the passage that it is worth presenting at some length:

My soul, so far as I understand it, has very kindly taken colour and form from the many various modes of life that self-will and an impetuous temperament have forced me to indulge in. Therefore I may say that I am free from original qualities, defects, tastes, etc. What I have I acquire, or, to speak more exactly, chance bestowed, and still bestows, upon me. I came into the world apparently with a nature like a smooth sheet of wax, bearing no impress, but capable of receiving any; of being moulded into all shapes. Nor am I exaggerating when I say I think that I might equally have been a Pharaoh, an ostler, a pimp, an archbishop, and that in the fulfilment of the duties of each a certain measure of success would have been mine. . . Intricate, indeed, was the labyrinth of my desires; all lights were followed with the same ardour, all cries were eagerly responded to: they came from the right, they came from the left, from every side. But one cry was more persistent, and as the years passed I learned to follow it with increasing vigour, and my strayings grew fewer and the way wider.

While scarcely managed with philosophical rigor, the argument is well-conceived, artfully written, and consistent with the larger concerns of the novel. Despite the powerful and persuasive image of the sheet of wax, Moore does not contend here, as many readers have supposed, that his narrator is simply the product of all the cultural forces in play, the final result of all his experiences (after all, even to be a sheet of wax is not to be nothing). On the contrary, there seems to be a dialectic of forces between "the many various modes of life" and the "self-will and an impetuous temperament" which engage in such life-choices. One is immersed in chance events, to be sure; but the way one responds to events is a pattern of character not traceable to the events themselves unless one is so devoid of personal energies that no response is possible. Hence the aboriginal "I" who makes these claims can assert that he would have been successful whatever his career, whether Pharoah or ostler, or the pimp or archbishop linked together by Moore with comic satisfaction. With his emphasis on the individual, Moore would hardly endorse a theory that stresses the overwhelming influence of the environment to the total extinction of personal force; his formulations here owe something to Schopenhauer, an influence present in much of the novelist's work of the period. According to Schopenhauer, will is objectified in the world, which affords a mirror to the man who will look into his life and see the manifestation of self under the various guises presented by experience. Perhaps unsurprisingly, this is exactly the program of *Confessions of a Young Man.*

The inclusion of Schopenhauer's view on the relationship between a man and his life is justified not only because it explains a great deal about the development of the narrator, Edwin Dayne, but also because it explains much more about the intent of this disguised autobiography. Moore in *Confessions of a Young Man* makes a novel about his own life; Schopenhauer claims that any biography is already a sort of novel, in which one may read the constant themes of an individual consciousness at grip with the diverse complexities of existence. A liberating idea, indeed, this becomes for Moore, who from this point is to write a host of books with titles using words like "Memoirs," "Reminiscences," "Avowals," "Conversations," "Communication," in which the fictional impulse runs in two directions at once—backwards to the reconstruction of the potential narrative found in experience, and forwards to the imaginative projection of the elusive personality who has suffered and enjoyed it all, yet only partially understood it. People like Yeats, who were to feel victimized by such published retrospections, complained that Moore was inclined to lay violent hands upon ascertainable facts and deform them to subjective and partial judgments. While probably well founded on human grounds, criticisms of this sort subtly miss the artistic mark in that they ignore the accord between theme and incident which gives coherence to the account from a point of view quite different from their own.

A consideration of the point of view of such recollections is always important because really there is no other, essential formal principle demanded by the genre—a memory has no shape but that given it by the one who remembers; in this it is quite different from histories or amassed public records, on the one hand, or from a sonnet on the other. Sometimes Moore's autobiographic work follows a more or less consistent chronological line, as in *Confessions of a Young Man*. Equally it may take the outward form of a collection of essays, of a series of conversations, of a series of specific reminiscences linked in the same way as a collection of short stories. But always two things are present: the narrator discovering himself by comparing different temporal perspectives, and a highly critical intent which develops as he detaches his vision of himself from the local conditions of culture which enclose it. One process is the correlative of the other. He must make himself as distinct as possible from the larger movements and pressures which comprise the peculiar tenor of the age, a task only to be accomplished by defining and finally passing judgment upon such tendencies. From the frequency with which he returns to personal delineation one would conclude that Moore is comfortable speaking about himself (which is a matter of purely psychological interest), but also that the freedom from formal restrictions is artistically congenial and fruitful and a genuine liberation from the necessity of belonging to a "school," whether of Zola or Balzac or anyone else.

Confessions of a Young Man, then, is the novel in which Moore most clearly declares his artistic independence. As later became evident, the book can be a trap and a puzzlement for critics. Written mostly in an intermittent present tense, the narrative does not reach the actual time of writing until the last chapter; this perplexing technique can make historical transitions of opinion seem like flat contradictions: Edwin Dayne offers two quite different views on the Impressionist movement, two on Zola, three on Shakespeare. A further difficulty is to be found in the style, which is not continuous or homogeneous in texture. One chapter in particular, "The Synthesis of the Nouvelle Athenes," is a series of jottings, notes of conversations which resemble a list of aphorisms of the kind favored by Schopenhauer: "Art is not nature. Art is nature digested. Art is a sublime excrement"; "Will the world learn that we never learn

anything that we did not know before?" "Art is the direct antithesis
to democracy." A history of one's education is of necessity a history
of mental events, of opinions changing constantly even while fundamental convictions and abilities do not change. The best, indeed
only, way to read this novel is to look for the consistent pattern that
explains the untidy event, and to recognize that for Moore education is a matter of growth of personality from the obscure instinct to
public act, not the passive reception of superficial instruction.

A boy hears his parents discussing a popular novel; he reads *Lady
Audley's Secret* himself, and then he turns to other works by Mrs.
Braddon, finally reading *The Doctor's Wife* and adopting its
heroine's love of Shelley merely because the sound of the name is
pleasing. His love of Shelley leads to freethinking and he is expelled
from the last school he is ever to attend. This apparent sequence of
chance occurrences is of considerable thematic importance. As autobiography, excepting the romanticized version of his departure
from school, the account is accurate enough. Moore did read Mrs.
Braddon early, and her influence can be detected throughout the
first half of his career, through specific details from *The Doctor's
Wife,* in *A Modern Lover* and *Esther Waters* and through the use of
the morally problematic hero seeking a decisive role in life. Yet it is
not the particular circumstances that are of interest so much as the
logic of their combination. Another boy would not have read these
books, or, reading them have been so impressed; he would not
likely have made the unusual transition to Shelley (why not to
Byron, also cited?); and no doubt he would not have made the
display of Shelleyan disbelief with the results indicated. The point is
that the accidental is a delusion; one's fate is already sealed with
one's personality.

The young Dayne's exclusion from formal education is for him a
constant theme. Speaking of his real artistic education, which took
place not at a university or art schools (despite his attendance at
Kensington and Paris studios) but in Parisian cafes, he says "I did
not go to either Oxford or Cambridge, but I went to the Nouvelle
Athènes." This is a development of an idea mentioned earlier that
his was the education of a "natural man," who allows his mind to
develop in the open air of modern life, as distinct from the "university man," who allows his mind to be filled by old ideas worn thin by
public usage. Again, he is to criticize his colleague and sometime
friend Marshall because Marshall is a product of education in the

modern sense of permitting a great deal to be put in, rather than in the older sense of drawing out what is already there.

If education is a matter of concentration, of preserving the essentials and casting away what is of no service, then the process of excoriation is almost as important as the process of consolidation. The Irish landlord who arrives in Paris to appropriate whatever is to be learned in order to be a painter, but accompanied by all the paraphernalia of the man of property, including a manservant from County Mayo who is not at all gratified to be in such alien surroundings, is a comical figure because he has not yet learned what must be retained and what must be cast away. The path of Dayne's progress in art soon comes to intersect the road of his social decline: to hear strong opinions from those doing artistic work of value, he has to abandon the Rue de Rivoli for the cafés; as he sinks progressively lower in cafés of less and less fashionable esteem he encounters progressively more distinguished (and more unpopular and more penurious) craftsmen; finally he finds a place in the sand-carpeted Nouvelle Athènes, around him assembled all the disreputables—Manet, Dégas, Pissarro, Villiers de l'Isle Adam, Catulle Mendès. Even this is not enough; not until increasing difficulties in Ireland effect a constriction of his income does he retire to a poor apartment in England and begin sustained work. Birth for the artist requires the death of the Mayo landlord. Similarly, each new opinion, every fresh acquisition of power, implies the ceasing to be of the opinion or mode of life that preceded it. Friends are used and cast aside, a new exile is chosen (three times!), past versions of oneself are laughed over.

It is just such a comic reappraisal that ushers in Dayne's picture of his reappearance in London: "Naturalism I wore round my neck, Romanticism was pinned over the heart, Symbolism I carried like a toy revolver in my waistcoat pocket, to be used on an emergency." The language of dress, always a symbol for Moore of the vapid and superficial, makes it clear that what is being treated lightly is not only the absurd young man, but also the schools which he espouses. Art, as Dayne remarks elsewhere, is personal emotion, right or wrong in proportion to its intensity; never is it the product of a coterie or group. It weakens as it becomes more widespread. To concentrate on essentials one must cast aside past ties quickly and ruthlessly. Inevitably the act of casting away from the old leads to moral paradox, just as it had seemed for Alice Barton in *A Drama in*

Muslin: it leads also to apparent duplicity and sometimes real contradiction, the espousal of Romanticism as well as Symbolism and Naturalism. Consequently there are many examples of conscious or unconscious hypocrisy in the novel, whether through a fleeting reference to Hugo weeping for the plight of the people at the same time he is cadging coppers for himself, or through an analysis of the conventions of the "Villa," which insists on absolute chastity in print, while remaining notably tolerant of actual scandal in its own midst.

But the best instances of duplicity are to be found in Dayne himself. Why does he come to dislike Marshall? His own explanation, "he allowed me to feel that I was only a means for the moment," is tantalizing because although it undoubtedly is a true statement, yet it depends for its force on its relationship to an earlier statement by Dayne about Marshall: "There was much that Marshall could teach me, and I used him without shame, without stint. I used him as I have used all those with whom I have been brought into contact." Dayne's hypocrisy here is a form of rage at seeing himself in the mirror, to use Wilde's phrase; it is part of the pain inherent in the transactions between the self and the world. In fact, many similarities are to be observed between the two: the Dayne who arrives in Paris with manservant and fine attire, a sort of dandy of art, is not so different from his colleague Marshall with his taste for exotic decor—the salon stretched with cloth like a Turkish tent, another room appointed like a Buddhist shrine. Dayne and Marshall exist like reciprocal possibilities of the same personality. Dayne fails as a painter because he lacks facility, no matter how hard he works, while Marshall, with evident skill and mastery in technique, fails through want of application. Marshall is able to offer such a clear contrast because he has become mentalized; he has found his place in the novel only through his evident relationship to the narrator. (This is a favorite effect for Moore. Even as early as the poem "Ode to a Beggar Girl" the cynical young narrator is fascinated by the young girl as an alternate potential self; later Moore is to structure *Hail and Farewell* on just such complementary pairs of personalities.)

Hypocrisy, as it is delineated in *Confessions of a Young Man*, is as much an intellectual as an ethical defect, for it consists, in the first instance, of the simple inability to perceive something true about oneself. This is not the whole story, of course, because behind the temporal blindness presented in such incidents is the comprehensive act of vision, of second-order awareness which tells the whole story in the completed novel. Nevertheless, for the reader there is a real difficulty in fixing upon the exact tone of certain passages, in which it is unclear whether one is meant to respond directly to the opinions of the garrulous and engaging speaker, or to see beyond these opinions to the older memoirist who recites them only to place in ironic context that absurd young man of so long ago.

In one well-known outburst, for example, Dayne complains against the reduction of rents from his property, arguing that it is monstrous that a few peasants should refuse to starve and so keep him from his comfortable life in Paris. Of this account, the distinguished biographer Joseph Hone notes "the anti-humanitarian principles of the Rue de la Tour des Dames were not put into practice on the estate," a comment that settles the issue so far as George Moore is concerned, but scarcely at all for Edwin Dayne.[1] Since there is throughout the novel a narrative prejudice that self-indulgence is incompatible with artistic creation, one assumes that there is criticism here of the frivolous aspects of Edwin Dayne, who can prefer his lurid Paris apartment complete with python to the intense industriousness which would ally him to those hungry farmers rather than to the idleness of a mere fop. But other parts of the text are more uncertain, as in the acceptance of the pagan world even to the point of wishing that a hundred gladiators would die if it were the price of washing away his Christian soul with their blood. Even admitting the formulaic nature of the statement (a somewhat similar comment is made elsewhere in the novel about Ingre's painting La Source being obtained at the cost of a young girl's virtue), and the constant brandishing of the idea that selfishness is redemptive, still the violence in the eagerness to shock cannot easily be explained. If this is a joke, it is a very odd one. Perhaps one is to fall back again into the realization that one is dealing with a very subjective view of the universe, a view with scarcely any "objective" force, consistent with the repeated suggestion offered by Dayne that art has value in direct proportion to its intensity, and that the criticism in the novel is not axiomatic, but only the expression of an individual taste.

A detail not to be forgotten in examining the profoundly individual taste of Edwin Dayne is that the career of this failed painter but successful novelist is the life of an artist. Moore here and everywhere feels that the genesis of an artist is the result of a certain kind of sensibility rather than the product of a certain kind of taste. It is, of course, an unquestionably post-Romantic conviction to espouse, but it has peculiarly Moore-esque features which are worth citing. Noting the difference between Marshall's attitude to pleasure and his own, Dayne is conscious of the contrast between his friend's ability to live in the present with a luxuriant ease and his own inability to forget the ticking of the clock. Just as in *A Modern Lover* the true artist is marked not only by his freedom from indulgence but equally by his lucidity about the phenomenon of time, by his awareness that there is a special relationship between art and change. Throughout *Confessions of a Young Man* there is a continuing dialog between two opposing impulses: the nostalgic appeal for the past as exemplified in Walter Pater's *Marius The Epicurean*, a book filled with unaffected joy in the living of life, and the need to find new forms tinctured by the hues of contemporary life. Robert Louis Stevenson and Henry James, two writers subjected to hostile judgments by Dayne, are dismissed because they have been crippled by their time. Dégas, on the other hand, is commended for his successful use of the cynical tone which is the insistent note of his age. Yet Dayne's first publication after he settles to a regular literary life in London is a series of poems about a sentimental yearning for the past—a past achieved at the cost of the deliberate rejection of the present. This indeed for Dayne is the artistic predicament, to be drawn to a condition of the permanent enjoyment of life, a condition which is necessarily unobtainable given the disposition of the artist. The solution to these difficulties is perhaps to be found in Dayne's appreciation of a painting by Pissarro of girls gathering apples: "That garden is the garden of the peace that life has not set for giving, but which the painter has set in an eternal dream of violet and grey." Art makes permanent pleasures which, in experience, cannot satisfy because of their fleetingness: this is the great discovery made by the Irishman after his attempts to balance the appeal of Marius and the challenge of Naturalism—"Art is eternal!"

Moore was always erratic in his response to criticism. Often uncertain in his confidence in his work, he could be outraged or downcast by what he read in the press; a curious reaction, this was, after all, for one who loved to provoke the Philistine. *Confessions of a Young Man* sold well and was widely reviewed, though with varying levels of appreciation. *The Academy's* reviewer returned to the attack with the question of why such an evidently disagreeable young man with no education should want to write his memoirs.[2] Curiously, Moore was unperturbed to the extent of telling his brother that all the reviews had been enthusiastic, a remark otherwise incomprehensible except for two warm letters from Walter Pater, who praised the originality of form, but drew attention to the book's "questionable moral shape."[3] The novelist was delighted.

III   Esther Waters

Between *Confessions of a Young Man* and *Esther Waters* Moore published a play, two volumes of criticism, three novels, and well above a hundred and eighty articles and short stories. As a crotchety elderly man of letters he was to be seen as a cautious and lapidary figure, revising work already done, but this accounting from a period of only six years shows that he could be capable of prodigious industry when he chose. During this time his periodical appearances show him to have been concerned with prudery and freedom in literature, the prospects of artistically valid theater in England, painters and their work (some of this later incorporated into book form), and his changing attitudes to Continental writers, most of all to Zola, Balzac, and Turgenev. Always remaining conscious of the importance for him of Zola in his early career, Moore nevertheless became caustic in his references to the pencil-and-notebook attitude to reality he had come to associate with Naturalism; he was newly impressed by the freer attitude of Balzac's realism; but still, he found newer sources of inspiration than these older masters in two writers, Edouard Dujardin and Ivan Turgenev. Dujardin, soon to become a close friend, had just written a book titled *Les Lauriers sont coupés*, a sort of combination novella and prose poem which scholars have taken as an important document in the development of what is called "stream of consciousness" technique. Moore was immediately enthusiastic, perhaps less from the invention of the method, already used by him in *A Mere Accident* (although the delayed publication of this novel renders it at least possible that Moore was influenced during the final stages of writing), than the abandonment of the "public" view of life for the interior life of the soul as the total perspective of the novel. It was a long time before Moore gave up his depictions of appearance and milieu (after all, there was abundant sanction for such description in Balzac), but even in the eminently solid *Esther Waters*, the life of the "Big

House" is presented only through the eyes of the newly hired servant girl. Moore met Turgenev only once, at a dance at which the still young Irishman was more interested in the ladies than hearing the Russian's opinion that in description it is more important to be aware of mental life than perspiration in the subject. Still Turgenev was to be a lifelong favorite and a convenient banner whenever Moore remembered his conversion from Naturalism.

Esther Waters is one of many books by Moore in which the central character is a woman. The character Esther is a figure who appears as a prototype in several earlier books: Gwynnie Lloyd in *A Modern Lover*, "Awful Emma" in *Confessions of a Young Man*, and others.[4] Yet the story itself, an account of the life of a servant, seized Moore soon after the writing of *A Drama in Muslin*, according to *A Communication to My Friends*, the last of the autobiographies. There are many similarities between the two novels. Both rely heavily on social analysis, but *Esther Waters* focusses on the life of the lower classes and treats the gentry as silhouettes, a reversal of the procedure of *A Drama in Muslin*. Esther is not as able as Alice Barton to draw the analogy between the lot of women and the inequities of the social structure, but there is nevertheless a clear suggestion of such a pattern in the narrative itself (most of Esther's difficulties come from men, usually perceived as violent or unreliable; instinctive, unselfish goodness is a possession exclusively of a few women). Esther is like Alice, too, in having the personal force to make her life harmonize with the integrity of her own character, in that her compromises are practical rather than ethically deforming: she is allied rather to Edwin Dayne than to Lewis Seymour. For Alice, the great problem is adjusting to the mysteries of sexuality and birth, while Esther's maternity becomes the central fact of her life as she fights for the life of her child (in the original, serial, version the story begins with Esther's pregnancy; Moore considered naming the book "Mother and Child").

In later life Moore alternated between genuine and mock sentimentality in recalling the tone of his novel, an ambivalence no doubt due to the social benefits alleged to have been produced by readers shocked at the fate of the unwed heroine, who is pressed to send her child to the untender mercies of a baby farmer. Ever at pains at the time to point out that his novel was a result of his love of the English disposition—"How I love that dull-witted race!"—yet the novelist included an enormous amount of material derived from his Moore

Hall experiences as a boy; even material, as Janet Egleson Dunleavy points out, oddly and distinctively unEnglish.[5] In fact the sentimentality and the Englishness seem to be pretty much the same thing. Moore is following a tradition reaching from Daniel Defoe through Samuel Richardson to Charles Dickens in the sympathetic depiction of the hurtfulness of lower class experience without any great concern for practical improvement of that experience, an attitude that is precisely sentimental. Hence the intent is to produce an English novel, even though the raw stuff of creation is Irish. It is not clear whether the novelist knew that the Plymouth Brethren were originally an Irish sect when he made his heroine a member of that denomination (though he could, in any event, have got his best information about the Brethren from his time in Dublin), but the thematic importance of the group is to supply part of that Protestant consciousness which Edwin Dayne in *Confessions of a Young Man* had said made England a great country. Mrs. Barfield, herself a member of the Brethren, calms her son's ire at the scruffy people invading his house for services by saying "the folk that you despise are equal in His sight." This subtle redressing of the misproportion between religious and social hierarchies is worthy of Samuel Richardson, significantly a writer esteemed by Moore as one of the founders of the psychological novel.

In 1901 Max Meyerfeld suggested that *Esther Waters* might well be a better novel than Richardson's *Pamela*.[6] Whether Moore had ever read *Pamela* is a fair question, but similarities do abound with Richardson, particularly in the simple triumph of goodness at the end of Esther's career. This triumph was rare for Moore, who was seldom interested in the purely ethical side of life. Yet as the comparison with *A Drama in Muslin* suggests, it simply will not do to exaggerate the unique status of *Esther Waters* as Moore's English novel. As a sort of triumph from his recent victory over the censorious libraries (a battle which involved the somewhat comical intrusion of Gladstone, who sent a postcard in support of the novel's moral tone), Moore was prone to say at the time that *Esther Waters* "radiates goodness"; a remark which, if true, admits him to the fellowship of Dickens rather than Zola. Later on, however, he was careful to distinguish between the effect of the book and his own intentions in writing it. As a brief survey of the novel will show, Esther's life is a far from unambiguous vindication of a life of virtue.

"She stood on the platform watching the receding train." Thus the novel opens not only with a vision of a train, an image used several times in the narrative, but with the more specialized picture of a disappearing train, a picture associated with other suggestions on the same page of recession, decline, and futility—the "barren country," the "decaying shipyards," Esther's own "faded yellow dress." It is as if this beginning were already a sort of death, as if the repetition of event and motif in the novel were a symbol of the ineffectiveness of human action. The fact that Esther is to return to the same station and the same house at the end of the novel intensifies this effect and leaves the reader with a feeling quite different from the satisfied sense of completion of many works of Victorian fiction. Very few of Moore's characters seem able to take much joy in life, their abnegation in this respect being almost an index of their integrity and a link with the melancholy disciples of Schopenhauer in Moore's first poems. (As a possibly unconscious reminder of the notoriety of *Flowers of Passion*, the printer decorated some copies of the first edition of *Esther Waters* with a spray of passion flowers on the cover.)

Driven into service by a brutal stepfather, Esther Waters finds several positions, even at one point as a maid for an "immoral" lady, before securing a place at Woodview, the Barfield country house in Sussex. There she falls in love and becomes pregnant by a servant named William Latch. He runs away with young Peggy Barfield, leaving Esther to conceal her condition to avoid dismissal. Inevitably, of course, the discovery is made; Esther is summoned into the presence of the kindly but now severe Mrs. Barfield, who banishes her with a small disbursement to pay toward her confinement. Already the novel is moving from the morally conventional to the ethically problematic: Esther was able to find her position at Woodview on the basis of a recommendation by Lady Elwin, written to rescue her from the atmosphere of the immoral house; but the final result of Esther's removal is to subject her to the attractions of William Latch. In effect, two stereotypes of moral conduct are placed in juxtaposition, that of Lady Elwin, who feels that vice is best cured by a removal of the evils of poverty in a rustic setting of association with refined people, and that of the Plymouth Brethren, who see riches as in themselves corrupting. This is a discussion which is continued throughout the novel; but it is a discussion from which Moore prescinds, for he refuses to condemn Esther, seeing her as betrayed, even as a betrayed heroine: "Hers is an heroic adventure if one considers it: a mother's fight for the life of her child against all the forces that civilization arrays against the lowly and illegitimate." Here, as in many other places, Moore makes a clear choice for human goodness, as distinct from goodness defined by codes of conduct or theoretical principles, which are often alienating and inhuman.

In London Esther stays with her mother and stepfather until it is time to go to the hospital, spending a little at a time on the choice cut of meat or bottle of beer which will placate the old man during her stay, each day doling out more of her needed money. As a result, when the child is born—she is now almost without funds—Esther is forced to leave Jackie with a baby farmer while she finds a job as a wet nurse; she does not realize until it is nearly too late that the system of baby farming means sure death for her child. Here Esther's instincts assert themselves, and she chooses to go to the bottom of the economic heap and live in the workhouse for a while, rather than sacrifice her child's life while caring for a rich woman's baby. After many difficult years with grasping employers, Esther does learn to adjust to a life controlled by the "dear gold"; finding at last in Miss Rice a considerate employer, she insists on a salary of eighteen pounds, knowing from experience she can survive on sixteen. The two women are not unlike and get along very well. Indeed, Esther's most satisfactory relationships are with two women, Miss Rice and Mrs. Barfield; not all women in the novel are so gentle or undemanding, but in general it is the men who are prone to force one into uncongenial paths by force or lies.

Just as Esther is settled with Miss Rice, another unsettling figure, a man, comes into her life. Fred Parsons is an unprepossessing man, but his life is bent by the violence of a few religious ideas: as a shop clerk his aggressiveness in directing customers to the Kingdom of Christ led to his dismissal; now he is just as avidly bent on reclaiming Esther to the Plymouth Brethren. Esther plainly sees Fred's limitations, but is attracted by his steadiness and by religious affinities, which, according to Moore, are as powerful as racial affinities. The reemergence of William Latch puts an end to this romance, however, for it becomes evident that Jackie will never consent to live happily in another man's house, once having met his own father. William, at this time, is still married; in order to supply evidence for the divorce, Esther agrees to live in William's public house. While never ceasing to be a naturally good person, Esther is forced to take positions that are morally neutral or even reprehensible with regard to public standards of morality. (After all, one concludes, this insistence on the absolute rightness of instinctive behavior is closer than at first appears to the casually arrogant self-assertiveness of *Confessions of a Young Man.*)

For a while Esther is happy in her new role as landlady of a tavern, just as she had been happy with Miss Rice, just as she had learned to feel at home at Woodview: in this novel one is permitted to feel secure at home no longer than Sinbad. But trade begins to decline and William encourages business by taking bets at the bar, an illegal undertaking which attracts the attention of the Salvation Army, then the police, then the courts. Faced with the loss of his license, William becomes a travelling bookmaker at the racecourses, leaving Esther in charge of the pub; but his health deteriorates under the open weather. With William's death Esther is for a last time obliged to find a position again at Woodview, where she lives alone with Mrs. Barfield, who, like Esther, spends a great deal of time worrying about her absent and now fully grown son. Esther's last conversation in the novel concludes this long recital of isolated triumphs of integrity surrounded by long and discouraging wastes of insecurity and disappointment. They are courageous but somehow sad and delusory words:"There's a good time coming; that's what I always says. . . ."

In *Esther Waters* success in the "little world" of private aspiration and personal integrity is balanced against success in the "big world," where other qualities are valued; hence Esther falls to the bottom of the social order in choosing the workhouse by precisely the same act of concern for the life of her child which gives her moral stature. As with Schopenhauer, chance is very powerful in the world: but in the things that matter—art, personal goodness—it is individual personality that counts. With natures of less energy, the role of chance (fate, genetics, social condition) is of proportionately greater importance; consider this first view of William Latch:

She looked and saw a low, narrow forehead, a small, round head, a long nose, a pointed chin, and rather hollow, bloodless cheeks. Notwithstanding the shallow chest, he was powerfully built, the long arms could deal a swinging blow. The low forehead and the lustreless eyes told of a slight unimaginative brain. Regular features and a look of natural honesty made William Latch a man that ten men and eighteen women of twenty would like.

Latch's fate is already in his anatomy. The weakness of the chest already suggests the early death from consumption; the lustreless eyes warning of an unimaginative brain foretell the narrow circling between tavern, women, and gambling which is to be William's life; the "look" of honesty predicts his attractiveness to the opposite sex, as does his generally powerful physique. In the hint that perhaps not quite so many men as women will find Latch likeable there is not only a qualification of that "look" of honesty, but actual book-maker's odds on his probable good fortune in future relationships with women.

Schopenhauer's view that life is divided into two halves, the sub-jective half which is invariable, and the objective half, which is chance, is associated in *Esther Waters* with the central metaphor of gambling. At every juncture weddings are promised for the time of expected race victories, and inevitably postponed when the horse refuses to cooperate; William declares his love for Esther at the celebration for the victory of Silver Braid at the Chesterfield Cup; the decline of the formerly wealthy Latches is said to be the result of horse racing; and William, like a true gambler, contrives to expire at the same time as the end of the flat racing season. At the end of his life William Latch again is the author of a wager, as he grimly bets for his life, hoping he can win enough money to save his health in Australia. Chance, according to Schopenhauer, is by definition un-avoidable, but they are most subject to chance who least assert themselves; the weak of character are the most prone to blame their luck—the vicious Bill Evans or more moderately unsteadfast Wil-liam Latch. In this connection it must be added that the love of Esther for William and of Sarah Tucker for the idler Bill Evans is itself a sort of wager, a hopeless, irrational investment unlikely to make return for the huge expenditure of affection and personal commitment.

Since chance is an external thing, it is not surprising that the controlling image often has a purely social aspect: when Esther complains that the system which compels her and her predecessor to neglect their own children in order to attend to the rich child is "two lives for a life," she is assessing the social parimutuel which weights the odds against the poor and hopeless. More than that, she is feeling the gratuitous nature of this convention, the mere, stupid game that controls the lives of all human beings. Power derives from social position, which is to say, from chance; the hypocritical judge, famous for his drinking and betting, who sentences Sarah Tucker for a crime "associated with the vice of gambling," is able to act as he does because of a social system based on blind hazard. The philosopher Jeremy Bentham envisioned a legal system so well proportioned that the criminal's very experience of it would tend to reform him; but in *Esther Waters* the judge is as guilty as the criminal. William makes a similar claim when he asserts that rich men may gamble in safety in their private clubs, a practice which earns him a stiff fine and a serious warning; and it is a practice, too, as William recognizes, different in neither intention nor effect from the respected operations of the stock market. In his recollections of the genesis of this novel in *A Communication to My Friends*, Moore emphasized the importance of the role of chance as conceived by sportsmen as an analogy for the social order, for he remembered that the treatment of Esther's life derived from his perception of similar attitudes evoked in the rich by the price of horseflesh and the eighteen-pound investment in a servant's salary.

Despite the fact that her training among the Brethren discourages her from countenancing with any favor the doings of the rich of this world, Esther is keenly aware of social differences allotted by chance, becoming sullen and resentful whenever her poverty or social standing is brought up against her—running out of the house when Mrs. Latch makes a caustic comment about her faded dress, or retorting in kind to Mrs. Rivers' supercilious comments to her new wet nurse. In the course of her life Esther manages to escalate her social position from kitchen maid at Woodview to, in her final place, also at Woodview, a sort of equal companion to Mrs. Barfield in an arrangement in which the two women come to live "more and more like friends and less like mistress and maid." Her quarters at the same time are removed from a tiny room under the eaves shared with another servant to a chamber in the main part of the house next to Mrs. Barfield's own room. Even now Esther's religious beliefs are pertinent because she shares with Mrs. Barfield membership in the Plymouth Brethren, just as together they had shared the cast-off clothes of Miss Mary in the time of their first acquaintance, with the result that the arbitrary differences between classes are subtly overcome.

When Esther achieves social parity with Mrs. Barfield during her final stay at Woodview, she is already the widowed Mrs. Latch, and her accession to social eminence of a kind is one more incident in the intersecting fortunes of the Latch and Barfield families. Formerly a distinguished house, the Latches have in recent generations fallen into servitude due to the improvidence and gambling of an ancestor; at the same time the Barfields rise from livery stable keepers to the proprietorship of Woodview. Further parallels abound. Not only is Esther like Mrs. Barfield, but correspondingly Mr. Barfield and William Latch lose a great deal of money racing, and both die of consumption; their sons, Arthur Barfield and Jack Latch, choose to live away from their families, visiting Woodview only occasionally. It is her association with William Latch that permits Esther to bridge the social abyss which separates her from the distant shore of secure existence. Taking William to meet his son for the first time, Esther from habit starts for the third-class carriage. But William, fresh from his life with Peggy, is used to travelling first class; in a neat act of compromise he steers Esther into the second-class carriage, thus artfully contriving her personal reconciliation at the same time as her class amelioration.

Old Mrs. Latch had hoped that William would be the one to restore the family fortunes; he, even as a boy, dreamed of keeping a tavern. Certainly for Esther The King's Head is a substantial promotion, one that almost admits of the quality of genteel proprietorship familiar from Woodview: "There would be a parlour behind the bar, in which she would sit. She would be mistress of the house. There would be a servant, a potboy, and even a barmaid." Between the two houses, Woodview and The King's Head, a curious relationship develops, each the mirror of the other as the center of a certain milieu: compare Mrs. Barfield's complaint "this house has been the ruin of the neighborhood, and we have dispensed vice instead of righteousness," with Fred's reproach about The King's Head, "this house is the immoral centre of the neighborhood. . . . " William's death brings to an end the little community at The King's Head; Esther returns to Woodview, and finds it, save for Mrs. Barfield, desolate also. (Both communities, as has been seen, have been reduced by the vice of gambling. With regard to the parallel between the manor hall and the public house, an interesting detail may be found in the account of the police raid on The King's Head, an account in which the perennial wastrels Joseph Stack and Harold Journeyman describe their occupation as "gentleman.")

If Esther's final attainment of a secure social position seems to show an ability to run with the moral hares and hunt with the worldly hounds as well developed as that of a Jane Austen heroine complacent in her virtue but rewarded with five thousand pounds a year, there is even more startling evidence to be adduced. Consider Esther's reaction to the recently truant William's disclosure that he is now worth three thousand pounds:

> At the mention of so much money Esther raised her eyes. She looked at William steadfastly. Her object was to rid herself of him, so that she might marry another man; but at that moment a sensation of the love she had once felt for him sprang upon her suddenly.

Or reflect on this conversation, soon after Esther has refused to marry William:

> "I can make that all right; I'll settle £500 on you and the child."
> She looked up; the same look was in her eyes, only modified, softened by some feeling of tenderness which had come into her heart.

Of course, a large part of Esther's gratification is to be explained by her concern for her son's future: it would not be just to accuse her of simple, self-regarding duplicity. Nevertheless, it does seem characteristic of her to seek a middle course wherever possible, to avoid the extreme configurations in which things are arranged in reality, whether in social organization or merely in her relationships with individuals (unable for a time to choose between Fred and William, she has a dream in which she marries both). Esther may be noble and self-sacrificing but she is not a fool; as aware as Schopenhauer of the unruly side of life governed by chance, she very early learns to manage her affairs so that she is not victimized again. There is, in fact, a sense in which the same sort of moral energy underlies good behavior and practical prudence, and it is this kind of energy that prevents her from falling into prostitution like her friend Margaret Gale. Margaret's explanation for her avocation is that she got into trouble through her employer and was forced out on the streets because, as a servant, "the better one behaves the worse one is treated, and them that goes on with service will find themselves in the end without as much as will buy them a Sunday dinner." Neither the circumstances nor the personal assessment are very different from Esther's own; Esther, eyeing the girls on Piccadilly Circus, sees them as much like herself—betrayed servants—but without the same ability to find positions.

Economically the relationship between servant and master does bear some resemblance to that between prostitute and client, as Esther finds when she learns that a servant must mask and disguise her own feelings in order to retain her place. In an early chapter Mrs. Latch even delivers the opinion that the function of servants is to lie and deceive when it is in the interest of the master, a confidential servant becoming the "Prince of Liars." But this ritual of concealment is not confined to the transactions between employers and retainers so much as constituting in itself a sort of law of life, for master and servant remain opaque to each other, with few exceptions. And just as often individuals remain opaque to themselves, unable to plumb the depths of subjectivity which are screened by habitual conceptions and the camouflages of social life. William Latch, for example, is unable to seize upon the similarities between himself and the "rotter" Bill Evans, who promises Sarah Tucker a home of her own and then abandons her (William had fixed his marriage to Esther at Woodview after the Leger; Bill Evans, just as unreliably, chooses the Cesarewitch for his nuptials). It must be added, too, that both William's victories over Esther seem to be due less to fate rather than to some unseen quality in Esther's character, for in each case, Esther, obviously the stronger personality, moves from active resistance to compliance. Conjecturally the answer may be found in the repeated detail that in each case William calls Esther his wife, her sense of a stable family being a permanently strong motive in her life. There is, in any event, a very strong psychologizing interest in the novel, a refusal to be satisfied with purely physical explanations of behavior, and a correlative determination to excavate the difficult quarries of human motive already partially explored in *A Drama in Muslin* and in the character studies in *A Mere Accident* (1887) and *The Strike at Arlingford* (1893). By a curious paradox, in this most English of his novels, Moore has completed an un-Saxon transition from a concern with what people do to how they think.

Esther Waters, in fact, has proved an exceedingly difficult novel to classify, partly indeed because it does represent a temporary point of consolidation in a journey between two modes of writing fiction. Critics at the time were sometimes misled by the banefully irrelevant. One complained of his disinterest in a book about servants; another (a sporting writer) became enraged at finding an apparent attack on horse-racing. While a good deal of reviewing paper was inevitably taken up by a discussion of the book's morality, still enough comment was enthusiastic to cause Moore to crow that he had silenced his enemies by writing a masterpiece. Both in popularity and esteem *Esther Waters* has survived perhaps the best among all of Moore's novels, although discussion has by no means ceased on the question of its Naturalistic intent or the related issue of its insistence upon a comparatively narrow sphere of experience. ("It is the most elaborate and learned study in literature of the English housemaid and barmaid and her environment" wrote Stuart Sherman in 1917 with much force and partial accuracy.[7]) It may well be that some portion of the artistic success of the novel is due to its very loose membership in any recognizable literary form or movement; Moore often succeeded best when his energies were given some freedom. His most memorable works—*Esther Waters, Confessions of a Young Man, Hail and Farewell,* among others—succeed with a suspension of the ordinary formal categories into which his work might be expected to fall.

IV   Spring Days, Mike Fletcher, Vain Fortune

If Moore believed he had produced a masterpiece in *Esther Waters,* he was perhaps due for one, having published between 1888 and 1891 three novels which occupy the lowest place in his canon, except for the early poetry. It is idle to speculate what it is in a work of art that stamps it is as a failure (or rather, save at the very lowest kinds of achievement, the reason is a psychological rather than a formal question), but Moore almost as soon as his critics perceived the limitations of these works. After calling it "the worst book I ever wrote," he somewhat inexplicably permitted *Spring Days* to appear in several revised versions until 1922; but *Vain Fortune* was allotted only one resurrection, and *Mike Fletcher* expired with its first appearance. To attempt to rehabilitate the reputation of these books is to perform an operation on a corpse, futile and bothersome. But as sources of insight into Moore's preoccupations and methods of this time the novels have considerable interest, particularly as they occasionally shed light on what is only obscurely visible elsewhere.

As early as *A Drama in Muslin* Moore had been promising to supplement his study of women in that volume with a companion book to complete the delineation of the era by an investigation of a group of young men (only Harding of the young men is also present in *A Drama in Muslin*). Although *Spring Days* and *Mike Fletcher* both resemble *A Drama in Muslin* in their Irish note—Harding, Frank Escott, and Mike Fletcher are Irishmen transplanted to London—they most closely resemble two other early novels, *A Modern Lover* with its development of the theme of the failed artist, and *A Mere Accident* with its investigation of bachelorhood. John Norton, the main character of *A Mere Accident*, does turn up again in *Spring Days* and *Mike Fletcher*. All three are to some extent romans à clef: John Norton is based on Moore's cousin Edward Martyn, Mike Fletcher on Augustus Moore and Frank Harris, Harding on a strange mixture of Moore himself and Zola's Fauchéry. *Mike Fletcher* is a sort of chronological continuation of *Spring Days*, but *Vain Fortune* is only thematically related. Not until *Hail and Farewell* will Moore produce a full-scale investigation of male relationships with the ambitious scope originally promised for these earlier novels: *Hail and Farewell* is the only undeniable success of this group, for Moore is often luckier with his female characters than with his male ones.

In *Confessions of a Young Man*, published a few months before *Spring Days*, the hero Edwin Dayne had expressed admiration for Dickens's novel *Bleak House* to a degree surprising when one considers the often marked dis-esteem for Dickens in other works. And the ambivalent fascination with money and rank in *Spring Days* and *Mike Fletcher* does suggest that in this first of the sequence of English novels which is to last until *Esther Waters*, Moore is writing a consciously Dickensian novel, minus the humor. Witness the scornful treatment of Chancery lawyers in *Mike Fletcher* and Mike's actual recollection of Mrs. Jellaby when he hears of a discussion of charities in India. It is useful to think of *Esther Waters* in this context because in the plan for the trilogy which *Spring Days* was meant to introduce, one volume was intended to be a study of servants from their own point of view, a point of view always present as one aspect of Dickens's work. In any event, much of the subject matter of *Esther Waters* is already to be found in *Spring Days* with its study of the "Big House," its weak characters complaining about their luck, even the scene in which a love relationship is decided by a choice of a railway carriage (unlike Esther, Frank Escott settles for third class).

A Dickensian novel for a man who has recently been lamenting the impotence of English letters is a difficult adjustment, to say the least. Critics who have uneasily found appropriate categories for

Esther Waters would do well to look at *Spring Days*, wherein the suspected tensions of the former book are magnified until they become openly discordant to a ruinous degree. A brief reading of the title page and preface promises "A Realistic Novel," a planned sequence of novels on the Don Juan theme, and an investigation of the "psychological interest" of this complex and strange idea of man. In other words, one is offered a work uniting the peculiar skills and frankly incompatible aims of Zola, Turgenev, and Balzac in the compass of a book directed at readers accustomed to Dickens and Jane Austen. Amid all this the allusions to the philosophy of Schopenhauer produce such an oddly miscellaneous effect that the harried reader can only echo the words of Frank Escott at the end of the novel, "Alas, those were Spring Days."

In a letter of 1888 Moore described Mr. Brookes of *Spring Days* as "a sort of comic King Lear," thus adding another source to the many influences at work (though one might still want to add Balzac's Old Goriot and Rastignac as the initial versions much watered down into Brookes and Frank Escott, particularly in view of the ending of the novel and Balzac's own allusions to Lear in *Père Goriot*). Brookes is financially successful, though a personally weak man unable to control his own daughters in their love affairs and reluctant to part with the money which will result in good marriages. His daughter Maggie falls in love with a likeable and quite untalented artist named Frank Escott, a young man with an expectation of inheriting the estate of Lord Mount Rorke. Frank, whose weak and foolish work is the inevitable result of a weak and foolish personality, has already broken a previous engagement because of a stipulation of Mount Rorke's that Frank marry a person acceptable as the future Lady Mount Rorke. A peculiarity of this novel is that while the characters are weak, money is strong, again and again extending its control over the lives of those who are brought into contact with it.

While acutely conscious of the will-rattling in Ireland, Escott lacks both the lucidity and the determination to act in any consistent program. He is the eternal husband figure for Moore precisely because he is so inconstant and unreliable, because he needs the reassurance of a settled existence. This is why the archetypal husband is, in fact, so remarkably inconstant a lover, unable to choose between Maggie Brookes and the bar girl Lizzie Baker to the extent that the mere absence of one means an attraction to the other. Marital faithfulness is nothing more than a willingness to escape permanently to the safety of one relationship following this view, and it is notable that Escott often uses the metaphor of "saviour" or "saving" for his love relationships, even going so far as to propose to Maggie as "he who shall save, the saviour who shall bring her home safe to the fold." Maggie does not look for redemption from a husband, and refuses Frank; but when he begins to act in a frenzied and helpless manner she later relents, sensing that she can save *him*. Two people sharing the peculiar notion that marriage is based on reciprocal helplessness may be supposed to have much in common; still, the course of even true love does not run smooth, and such strange affections are in for a much bumpier journey, particularly when a sick and dispirited Lizzie reappears on the scene and reclaims Frank's interest. Frank's engagement to Maggie Brookes is broken, and he returns to the pursuit of Lizzie Baker, Mr. Brookes realizes an old threat and sells the manor house, and all passes into indefinite dissolution.

In many ways *Spring Days* is a study of weakness, the mirror opposite of that other novel of apprenticeship, *Confessions of a Young Man*, which it in some ways resembles. Schopenhauer's repeated notion that what people call fate is generally nothing but their own weak and foolish natures is the rule upon which are constructed the roads and pathways of behavior for the helpless people in the novel; really there is nothing to choose between Willy Brookes's laments that luck has always been against him and Frank's exultant belief in faith or destiny. Mr. Brookes's Micawber-like refrain of helplessness, "I suppose it will be all the same a hundred years hence," is of a piece with Willy's financial ineptitude, Sally Brookes's passions for lower-class young men, or Maggie's hysteria when her affairs become disorderly. Nor is Frank the only person for whom money is overwhelmingly powerful in view of his own feeble energies: Willy is obliged to conceal an unsuitable marriage and live a double life in order not to lose his inheritance; like Frank again, Willy is only an intentionist, never able to carry an idea to a satisfactory conclusion, a defect as fatal in business as in art. As remarkable evidence of the potency of money compared with frail human force, consider this account by Brookes's pompous son-in-law Mr. Berkins: "The first twenty thousand is very uphill work, the second is on the flat, the third is going downhill—it brings itself along." Here a commonsense idea has been elevated to a sort of universal principle concerning the organic vitality of capital itself, which is far more decisive than the paltry physical or intellectual contributions of mere men. Certainly for Brookes himself the suggestion is a very persuasive one, for he already makes his judgments purely on fiscal rather than personal grounds, whether he complains of his daughters and their wasteful ways, condemns the villa crowd moving in because they lower property values, or remains strangely blind to the deficiencies of Berkins upon finding that Berkins is worth seven or eight thousand a year.

It is one of the ironies of this "Prelude to Don Juan" that men are relatively passive and dominated by their women; that Mr. Brookes, who himself often weeps and laments in a womanish fashion is the widower of the fierce Julia Brookes who used to chase him around the table with a carving knife; that Willy squanders his money and his chances in the effort to win independence for himself and his secret bride; that Frank Escott should endanger his inheritance in the pursuit of two not-very-attractive women. The family, or rather the psychology of the "family man," is the rock on which idealism is dashed to pieces. Only the comparative detachment of Lord Mount Rorke or the novelist Harding promises of genuine artistic or personal achievement, because this coolness is, in effect, requisite for the long views which are necessary for a lucid use of energy in the real world. Frank's habitual self-deception and incapacity for gauging the consequences of any action are the inevitable corollaries of his role as the dependent husband figure, for the role implies an inability to deal with life from a strong position, the need to find immediate compromises no matter how false. It goes without saying that the degree of Frank's success as a husband will preclude in the same measure any chance of success as an artist.

For the hero of *Mike Fletcher* the terms of existence are the same but the elected role is quite different. Meditating suicide at one point Mike reflects: "Ridiculous as a wife and children are when you look at them from the philosophical side, they are necessary if man is to live." This neat equation between life, marriage, and irrationality is the ideology not only of Don Juan, but of the potential suicide, the man who refuses to accept life on any terms but his own. Mike Fletcher is the Don Juan promised in the preface to *Spring Days*, but as such he is a nineteenth-century anachronism, born out of his time and doomed to a tragic end; he is a reminder of the freer sensuality of Greek antiquity degraded and transformed like Yeat's Helen in "No Second Troy." Frank Escott seeks permanent relationships with women because he is unable to deal with life; Mike avoids permanent arrangements because he will not accept life as it is. Just as Frank is the perfect husband precisely because of his own weakness and inconstancy, Mike becomes the lover of many through his own detachment and aloofness; the whole world may be in love with him, but he is utterly alone. When Mike does fall in love, it is with a woman who cannot love him, who soon dies of consumption and leaves him as solitary as before. Pure dependency and pure estrangement, the eternal husband and the archetypal Don Juan, Frank Escott and Mike Fletcher exist not only as friends and roommates in *Mike Fletcher*, but as human extremes related as opposites in kind often are related, as if one were a mere reformulation of the other, mutually implicated in the other's actions. Frank, now married to Lizzie Baker, reads in the newspaper that the new Lady Mount Rorke has been delivered of a son (and that therefore he no longer has a chance for inheritance) on the same day that Mike receives a letter telling him that one of his women friends has left him a fortune. And at this moment with his new money to bolster him, Mike sends a letter of proposal to Lily Young although he has before him the evidence of how marriage has ruined Frank Escott. When, inevitably, Mike tears up his fragile compact with life, it is to Frank Escott and Escott's illegitimate child that he leaves all his money.

When *Spring Days* appeared, Moore for once was genuinely shocked at the unanimity with which the critics condemned his book. Lamely claiming that he had been attempting to recreate the work of earlier English novelists, he promised that *Mike Fletcher* would be genuinely new in method, although he could not be sure that this first experiment would be a work of genius. His subsequent comment, after the failure of the American edition, that the fault of the book is its lack of order and development, hints that the presumptive new method is identical with the supposed defect later uncovered, that Moore was writing a book almost without plot in which the contrapuntal arrangement of characters in complex groupings substitutes for a conventional narrative line. Moore had been praising the work of Wagner for some time before this. His construction of a novel that is "all melody," in which the principal interest is the exfoliation of a few simple ideas developed into patterns by the characters who embody them under various guises was the first use of a technique to be used triumphantly in *Hail and Farewell* and all the later novels.

On another axis, the involved relationship of similarities and radical dissimilarities between Mike and Frank is reproduced again in
the alliance between Mike and John Norton, two friends who share
personal sympathies but part company in the matter of conduct;
Mike deplores John's fanatical religious conscience, while John condemns Mike's tendency to follow every passion. Both, however, are
pessimists and disciples of Schopenhauer, both speak of their conviction of the inferiority of women and the necessity for solitary
contemplation of one's own condition without the constant interrup-
tions of family life. Harding's appreciation of them as two halves of a
single personality, each inviting only a portion of experience has, of
course, a special application to this pair, but it also announces the
program by which character is delineated everywhere in *Mike
Fletcher*, a program of variations on the same theme. In their attitudes to love and sexuality, for example, Mike and John share a
closer range of views than might be expected for a permanent celibate and a philanderer. Mike finds all men hideously ugly, whereas
John is drawn by male beauty; yet both are motivated by a perception of the inaccessibility of the opposite sex, John remaining dis-
dainfully aloof while Mike pursues women precisely because they
present the challenge of the remote and mysterious. John's obsession with religion has a strongly sensual side to it (Lady Sevelely in
Spring Days said that "no sensuality is so terrible as religious sensuality"); he himself speaks of the "lust of eternal life". Conversely, the
perennial chase of women has an almost metaphysical, mystical,
side for Fletcher, who feels compelled to be with this sex "as a
shadow is with its object," as much in pursuit of a finally intangible
ideal as John is in toying with the symbolism of Popes, cardinals,
and religious architecture. On the whole, both men remain ineffectual for the same reason, too; for neither is able to be totally consistent in his practice. As the percipient Harding notes, there is something unresolved, something muddy, about John Norton's mind,
because the woman-hating Norton is able to accept without reserva-
tion all of Catholicism with its reverence for Mary. In much the
same way Fletcher finds for himself a struggle in which, by the rules
of the game, he cannot succeed, the attainment of the unattainable
ideal of femininity; he remains half a dreamer and half a man of
action.

Mike's attraction to the ex-nun Lily Young is, of course, a symp-
tom of the self-defeating side of his personality since Lily cares not

at all for him, or indeed for any lover whatsoever. She has left the convent, bringing with her, however the ideal of the "Divine Lover," whom she intends to seek in the world. In this ambition she unites the unattainable ideals of Fletcher and Norton. Like Norton she has abandoned life in the cloister to let the world be her convent (she always wears nun-like colors, usually gray or black); like Fletcher she has a very physically precise sense of the nature of the pursued lover. That she should be so ardently courted by Fletcher completes the implicit transactions between the two men, particularly in view of Mike's admiration for her because of her resemblance to Seraphita. Balzac's heroine is both spiritualized and bisexual (or asexual in the sense of transcending the categories of sex); Seraphita is a curious model of womanhood for the appetite of a celebrated libertine.

Lily's puzzling attractiveness for Fletcher is explained, in part by her similarity to John Norton, whose indifference to women takes on a particular form, as in this partly esthetic, partly sexual comment: " 'I never could think a female figure as beautiful as a male' . . . as he spoke his eyes followed the line and balance of Mike's shoulders." More than philosophical assumptions underlie the friendship between the two men. It has become a psychological commonplace that the sexual athlete is compensating for his own inadequacies; but how many people were saying this in 1889? Moore's investigation of "this idea of man, so complex and so strange, so full of subtle psychological interest" is as remarkably prophetic of later findings as his analysis of the Irish social scene in *A Drama in Muslin* and *Parnell and his Ireland* and his use of the stream-of-consciousness technique in *A Mere Accident*, and it is a vindication of the new methods announced in his plans for *Mike Fletcher*. Homosexuality implicit or explicit is ever a favorite topic for Moore, whether it is a question of Cecelia Cullen in *A Drama in Muslin*, Dolly and Beaumont in *A Mummer's Wife*, or "The Hermaphrodite" from *Pagan Poems*. In "The Hermaphrodite" homosexuality is perceived as almost a kind of sexless idealism, the yearning for "beauty untouched by the soiling/ Stain of a sex," a passion without a proper object; and thus it is akin to the indefinite yearning equally of Norton and Fletcher as well as of Lily Young.

John Norton's reconciliation of Christianity with the philosophy of Schopenhauer rests upon his conviction that "Jesus Christ Our Lord is the perfect symbol of the denial of the will to live"; his religion for him is overtly a sort of death wish, as is Fletcher's promiscuity. Lily inevitably fails to find her "Divine Lover" in the world, but on her death bed has a vision of her saint surrounded by "his Maries," and hastens to join him with the claim "I am his Mary, am I not dear?" It is the austerity of the demands of love for these three lovers which is so striking, a kind of love which is evacuated finally of passion in the immediate physical sense, and which reminds of Schopenhauer's turning to Eastern thought in old age. (John Norton's room contains an effigy of the Buddha; Lily Young's house becomes a meeting place frequented by Buddhists; Mr. Stokes, one of a group of Temple lawyers, is writing a book about Buddhism.) T. Bailey Saunders' characterization of Schopenhauer seems almost a deliberate evocation of John Norton, but when the necessary adjustments have been made it can be seen to have application to all the central characters of *Mike Fletcher:* "His heroes are the Christian ascetics of the Middle Age, and the followers of Buddha who turn away from the Sansara to the Nirvana."[8]

The invocation of Schopenhauer in this discussion of *Mike Fletcher* is not at all a superfluous suggestion, for never did Moore write a novel as insistently interlaced with the spirit and teachings of the German sage. Mike and John count themselves disciples of Schopenhauer, but this open partisanship is perhaps the least important of the uses to which this philosophy is put. Schopenhauer's dictum that birth is the greatest curse and death the blessedest relief of life is developed through many narrative details: the chosen suicides of Lady Helen and of Mike; the yearning for death by John, whose conscience, however, debars him from the necessary act; the misery brought to Escott and Lizzie by the birth of a legitimate heir to Mount Rorke and to Mike by the birth of his illegitimate child. Again, and most significantly, there is a decisive choice for the world of subjectivity over the world of random event: the refusal of the need to live is for these people the commitment of the will to realize itself.

The subjective half of life, which for Schopenhauer is the most important half, constantly triumphs in *Mike Fletcher* over the conditions of the objective half; the elimination rather than the acceptance of responsibilities is the goal of life in this novel, which is as much as to say that it is in intent a novel in which the overt actions of the characters are of minimal interest when weighed against the inner world of personal choice. A novel with only tangential and indirect involvement in the requirements of plot must have been a puzzling object indeed for the readers of 1889, who could scarcely be expected to share its author's enthusiasm for the philosophy of Schopenhauer or the stylistic experiments of Dujardin. In reality a *conte philosophique*, *Mike Fletcher* is, as Moore claimed, very different from the novels of Dickens and Thackeray, for it is inclined to suspend or treat lightly the very qualities which these latter writers take very seriously indeed, conventional narration and characterization. Characters are presented not as more or less concrete nodules of behavior so much as the realization of certain ideas, deriving their interest from the degree in which they represent these ideas. Harding's observation that John Norton and Mike Fletcher are detached halves of a potential whole personality serves equally well other pairs of characters who embody not consistent, physical and moral experience, but philosophical possibilities—Frank Escott and Mike Fletcher, John Norton and Lily Young, Lily Young and Lady Helen, the lawyers Silk and Cooper (one concerned only with matters of ethics, disregarding practical considerations; the other interested solely in securing legal briefs without any thought of moral principle; both are friends, both failures).

For its originality of conception and execution, *Mike Fletcher* is in every way a better work than *Spring Days*, although not up to the mark of *Esther Waters*. Still, Moore refused ever after to countenance *Mike Fletcher*, the only one of his novels not to be republished from this period, the one he tried most devotedly to forget. Critics and friends alike were put off by the book, although in England it did not fail financially; in New York the sheets were almost lost when the company that had accepted it went bankrupt, and on its first and only American appearance it contributed as well to the failure of the Minerva Publishing Company, which complained that no copies could be sold. A few months earlier Moore had spoken of *Mike Fletcher* as a "really great novel, quite first rate," had even spoken of a lecture tour of the United States consisting of readings from the same work; but his nervousness at the recent prosecution for obscenity of Henry Vizetelly, English publisher of Zola's work, coupled with his uncertainty at negative critical response and his real interest in the sales made him anxious to forget the book. Yet never the man to discard a useful theme or a technique capable of profitable retrieval, he made use of the formal pairing of characters in *Hail and Farewell* almost twenty years later in a memorable novel also devoted to the configuration of idea and personality rather than to the unwinding of a linear plot.

If there is a note that survives throughout Moore's career and all the stages in that career, it is his love for treading on the corns of the philistine, the man who lacks the capacity (and really it is a matter of character) to succeed in art. Hubert Price, the artistic failure in *Vain Fortune*, is too prone to bemoan his fate, other people, critics, for his shortcomings; too eager to find a formula for the road to fortune rather than to depend upon himself. His failure, of course, is internal rather than external, for he lacks both the capacity for self-sacrifice and the energy which are characteristics of the true artist. Like Flaubert's Bouvard and Pécuchet (frequently alluded to by Moore in *Hail and Farewell* as comic models for various among the personnel of the Irish Renaissance), his inefficacy is aboriginal; he is condemned through want of personal proficiency to offer a running parody of those who achieve real success in art because they are not distracted by the affairs of fortune.

The novel opens (as it ends) at night. A description of and comment upon some handwritten lines of a play, the hand that writes it, the dirty cuff that encases the hand, the coat that covers the cuff—all these precede the unimpressive appearance of Hubert Price half in light, half in darkness, "almost handsome," already taking a cigarette to release him from the labor of writing. The compromises suggested in this delineation of a man contained in, not dominating, his affairs, are amplified by the particulars of his handwriting: "The hand traced a few lines of fine, beautiful calligraphy, then it paused, correcting with extreme care what was already written and in a hesitating, minute way, telling of a brain that delighted in the correction rather than in the creation of form." This needs explanation. There seems to be immediately a connection between the eternally revising novelist George Moore and Hubert Price, who also specializes in revision: one could direct a shrewd guess that Moore's frequent use of the theme of the inadequate craftsman objectifies occasional doubts about his own capacities. But one needs to add also the Théophile Gautier, the poet and scourge of the bourgeois praised in *Confessions of a Young Man* and elsewhere, had said that virtue is the correction of form. Price is held accountable not because he corrects, but because his revisions substitute for rather than continue the creative process; the slenderness of his vigor is made clear in the telling adjectives "hesitating," "fine," "minute."

Futhermore, Price, it appears, spends ten times as long "dreaming" about a play than actually writing it. He is, as the ever-present Harding suggests, only an intentionist, unable to bring any idea to a satisfactory conclusion. Still seeking distraction from the task of working on his play, Price opens a copy of a weekly journal and finds an article about himself which expresses the need to hear from Price again after his first play, *Divorce*. Moore at this time was much involved in the writing of plays and of articles assessing, generally unfavorably, the condition of the theater in England; and save for the references to Price, the article conforms pretty well to the tone of Moore's theatrical criticism, particularly to an article titled "Our Dramatists and Their Literature" subsequently included in *Impressions and Opinions*. In this article Moore complains that the contrived melodramas and familiar plots of contemporary theater are not surprising because most of the people who become successful as playwrights have already failed as novelists, painters, and in other arts. The formula exactly fits Price, who has behind him several disastrous careers as painter, poet, and essayist, and who, even more tellingly, chose a life in art because he felt obviously unsuited to any of the professions. For Moore, the road to art takes one away from the crowd, possibly through poverty, certainly through isolation and estrangement from comfort. But for Price art is just a means to an end, the social and economic passport to leisure, fine women, an English home; and when he becomes discouraged it is because he feels that he has made a mistake, that his scribbling has separated him from what he nostalgically calls "life" (in which he apparently does not include art).

In the same boarding house on the Tottenham Court Road lives another struggling hopeful, the artist Rose Massey. Rose is to appear at crucial points in the novel because she serves as an ironic foil to Hubert; she is the young artist capable of "realizing her desire," as Moore puts it in a phrase strongly reminiscent of Schopenhauer. Faced with mounting debts, Hubert decides to make a clandestine departure and solve his problems with his disappearance: the gesture is a characteristic one, for he lacks the fixity necessary in art as in life. His new existence forces him to eat in a workingman's café as an economy measure which appalls Price, who hates the shifts of bohemian life enforced by the position of the artist in the nineteenth-century scene depicted by Moore in his art criticism. In the café Price meets another figure bearing a derisive resemblance to himself, a chalk pavement artist. This man has run against the tide of public taste as much as Hubert Price, but whereas Price has tried to introduce psychological interest to a theater audience accustomed to facile stagecraft, the virtuoso of chalk has replaced the traditional pictures of slabs of bacon and ships on fire with recreations of the works of Thomas Gainsborough and William Etty. Chagrinned that being too successful was his misfortune, the man recalls that enormous crowds gawking at his nudes provoked unwelcome police attention.

Reduced even further in his financial condition, Price works for a time as a laborer, but Moore is quick to point out that this toil is "not in contradiction to, but in full harmony with, his true nature"; Hubert's case is not so much a tragedy as a grim comedy on the order of the pavement artist's, because he is a pathetic, not a heroic, over-reacher. Price does think of his unfinished play, "The Gipsy," in these days, but it is in terms of the freedom a successful run of the play will mean for him rather than the possibility of completing a masterpiece. As his chances of ever working again at his play become more and more remote, Hubert grows more and more despondent and is, in fact, on the verge of suicide when he hears from Rose Massey that there is to be a revival of *Divorce* (the titles of Price's dramas *Divorce, An Ebbing Tide, The Gipsy,* are associated with the minimal, with withdrawal, escape, wandering).

The revival does not go well. *Divorce,* according to the critics of its first run, is carried by the strength of its first act. Yet as vain fortune will have it, people are still arriving and causing a distraction all through this part of the play. And the play itself is devoted to a study of the operations of fortune; the main character, Mrs. Holmes, is divorced because circumstantial evidence makes it appear, quite wrongly, that she is unfaithful to her husband. Mr. Holmes is an incorrigible rotter, a woman-chaser and a drunkard; finding his mistake, he begs his wife's forgiveness, even promising to commit suicide so that she can marry the man she loves, for she believes that marriage can only be dissolved by death. Of course, Holmes is too weak to carry out such a promise, and the play ends inconclusively and untidily. Even such a summary makes clear that the play is, inevitably, a failure. Yet in its evocation of the incorrigibility of character and the decisively malignant operations of fate, it is a true child of its begetter and even a prophetic statement, in view of

Price's future entanglements. Hubert is easily dashed or cheered by the expectations of others, a man always surprised to discover that occasionally friends believe in him more than he believes in himself; in his moment of gloom now he is the victim of that "public taste" which Moore in *Modern Painting* says is destructive of art.

Despondent once again to the point of suicide, he receives another visit from Rose Massey, who urges him to open a solicitor's letter on the table (Rose, like the irresistibly ascendant person she is, has managed to turn her small part in this lackluster play into a triumph). To Price's astonishment he is suddenly a rich man, for his uncle has unaccountably left him a great deal of property and considerable wealth. These rhythmic advances and recessions of prosperity are indeed vain, in the sense of arbitrary (the uncle's caprice that leaves Price a wealthy man also deprives the ward, Emily Watson, of her promised inheritance); but not in the sense of unaccountable. On the contrary, it is an iron law which chains a character to his fate, because one's own weaknesses or resolution of disposition constitute that fate. Among these three weak people, Mr. Burnett, Emily Watson, and Hubert Price, is spun a subtle but unbreakable web produced by the interaction of character: Emily's selfish and ineffectual love for Hubert is like Hubert's inconstant and futile affection for his art; the childish malice of Mr. Burnett for Emily derives from his inability to win her love. Hence the apparent random cycling of fortune whether for good or ill is powered by the totally consistent pattern of character that actuates it, a consideration which explains Moore's difficult comment in *Confessions of a Young Man*: "rhythm and inevitableness (two words for the same thing)."

A critic of *Divorce* had said that a fault of the play was that it was unrepresentative, that it fastened upon a rare case of unhappiness, ignoring the widespread contentment that is the general lot of people seeking marriage. Tested against the dramatis personae of *Vain Fortune*, the thesis is problematical. Emily's companion Mrs. Bentley has survived an unfortunate marriage; for Emily herself the passionate wish to marry Hubert leads to emotional disturbance and suicide, despite her own memories of her parents' quarrels; Mr. Burnett had suffered because of his attachment for Emily; Hubert's ultimate marriage to Julia Bentley seems from the outset an unpromising arrangement, darkened as it is by Emily's suicide and Hubert's divided allegiances. Thinking in his new estate of the prospects opened by new wealth, Hubert is uncertain of the best course: "he would like to marry; but perchance bachelorhood was the natural state of the artist." This, then, is the key that explains the discussion of marriage and links it to *Spring Days* and *Mike Fletcher*. The psychology of the eternal husband is ultimately antipathetic to the psychology of the eternal artist because one is always seeking rest and safety while the other is in search of challenge and activity. Price occasionally has the lucidity that Frank Escott lacks, is able to see that marriage is a temptation, a sort of shorthand for all those comforts from which the artist must abstain; nevertheless, he does marry, and the compromises adhering to this decision produce the same kind of unlovely complications as those associated with Mr. Holmes in his play *Divorce*.

In *Vain Fortune*, as indeed in various works by Moore *(Hail and Farewell, Spring Days)*, the country is related to the world of women and the peaceful enjoyment of life, the city to men and the world of work. Confined by poverty, Price dreamed of the leisure that would allow him to work as he might choose, yet when he does realize this wish on his new estate, he feels no compulsion to begin writing, reasoning that he can take as long as he pleases to finish the task. To complete the equation, Price at Ashwood is not only unable to work, but is drawn to a morass-like entanglement with Emily Watson and Julia Bentley (in the city he had no women friends, even spoke of his unattractiveness to women). Emily's evident passion for Hubert he soon comes to feel a distraction, sensing that she occupies time that might be filled by working on his play; and as she becomes more demanding he grows correspondingly cooler to her. Matters are not mended by Emily's jealousy of Julia Bentley, or by the fact that Hubert is better able to straighten out the quirks in his scenario by discussing them with Julia, who seems not to mind Hubert's sharing of affection between her and his craft.

In a difficult situation for which he wants the energy necessary to effect a decisive solution, he tries to escape from his problems again by physically removing himself, just as he had in his various moves in London. He elopes with Julia and goes to London to marry; they go to see Rose Massey, now acclaimed, in a play; returning to their hotel, they presently receive a letter telling of Emily's suicide. As Julia sleeps, Hubert thinks first with interest, then with discouragement of his play, and begins to meditate upon suicide again. Julia begins to stir, and the novel concludes in these words: "Pale and overworn, but in all her woman's beauty, she came, offering herself as compensation for the burden of life." Lovely as these words are, they are bitterly ironic, the final index of Price's failure, for they indicate that his marriage definitively substitutes for the burden of life, that it has become the effective sepulcher of his talent.

Vain Fortune was written during work on *Esther Waters*, a fact which may signal the lesser hopes Moore entertained for this book originally projected as a money-raising venture in its serialized appearance in the *Lady's Pictorial*. By the time *Vain Fortune* made its full-length debut, its author's estimation had evidently improved, since he had the book published in a large-paper, limited edition as well as the usual edition. Neither sold, the remainder sheets being used by another publisher the following year, and the critics, perhaps inspired by the novelist's very bravado, were very down on the book, although another Irish novelist, James Joyce, was to single out *Vain Fortune* for praise ten years later in his pamphlet, "The Day of the Rabblement." Latterly, the distinguished biographer Richard Ellmann has proposed *Vain Fortune* as a source of Joyce's long story, "The Dead"; the suggestion is a persuasive one, and it does seem probable that for reasons of personal affinity, historical contiguity, and the force and quality of the models of craftsmanship, Joyce was deeply influenced by the older man.[9]

V Celibates

As a penniless newcomer to Trieste, James Joyce tried to interest an Italian publisher in a proposed translation of *Celibates*, and indeed did translate the first chapter. The manuscript of this translation, now reposing in the Cornell Joyce collection, suggests that Joyce at the time overestimated his idiomatic command of Italian; certainly he overestimated the demand for this book, which to this date has never been published in Italian or by an Italian publisher, and it seems unlikely that it ever will be. Moore with justice regarded the book as fine work, but it has enjoyed little popularity, perhaps because its central concerns were of greater permanent interest to Moore than to his readers. *Celibates* is not one story but three: using the experienced craftsman's prerogative of reworking congenial materials into newer forms, Moore transformed his novel *A Mere Accident* into "John Norton," and revised "Mildred Lawson" from a previously published story titled "An Art Student"; only "Agnes Lahens" was written for the first time. And there are many familiar faces in the array of themes developed in this collection: the incompatibility between the life of art and settled, family existence; the hidden sensuality of intense religious experience; the problematic role of women in art; the tension between fruitful activity and the ability to enjoy life spontaneously.

The reader of *Celibates* is confronted by a collection of stories, not stories that are continuous in terms of plot, not stories written or conceived at the same time nor obviously identical in style. What is the model to be proposed for this kind of book? Moore had written a series of discontinuous sketches in *Parnell and His Island* in 1887 and was to do so again with notable success in 1903 with *The Untilled Field;* but these, while in some ways bearing affinities to *Celibates,* are books sustained by a single effort to delineate a specific cultural entity, Ireland. For *Celibates* there is no such unified subject, but merely a series of psychological studies of people who choose not to be married. Balzac, it is true, did group a number of novellas under the title *Célibataires,* but the grouping took place as an afterthought subsequent to the writing of the stories, which are frankly miscellaneous in form, and which, in any case, bear little resemblance to Moore's work (although Moore was familiar with Balzac's stories and possibly did borrow the title). Flaubert's *Trois Contes,* like *Celibates,* is a trio of tales concerning people whose experience in life is oversimplified, unprobed to the point of childishness; and Moore's exploration of religious sensuality does bear an undeniable resemblance to that of Flaubert. Nevertheless, *Celibates* most clearly derives from the novel sequence that includes *Spring Days, Mike Fletcher, Vain Fortune,* and, of course, *A Mere Accident* in terms of theme and technique: *Celibates* is, in fact, a condensed novel sequence in its own right. The man who waged such vigorous warfare in youth against the tripledecker novel retained a nostalgia for the triadic form, using it not only here but in *Hail and Farewell* and *Daphnis and Chloe.* Many of his other novels also have discernible tripartite narrative structure; no doubt Esther's return to Woodview at the end of *Esther Waters* is in part due to the sense of completeness conferred by this form.

It is the first of the stories from *Celibates,* "Mildred Lawson," that Joyce began to translate into Italian when he was living in Trieste. Idle as it may be to speculate why any motive beyond economic necessity urged Joyce to the selection of this work, it does seem that the style of the opening of the story links it more to the twentieth century than to the century in which it was written:

The tall double stocks were breathing heavily in the dark garden; the delicate sweetness of the syringa moved as if on tiptoe towards the windows; but it was the aching smell of lilies that kept Mildred awake.

As she tossed to and fro the recollections of the day turned and turned in her brain, ticking loudly, and she could see each event as distinctly as the figures on the dial of a great clock.

Omitting as quickly as possible without actual haste the question of whether the visualization of the clock face is the source of the image used in the famous discussion of "epiphanies" in Joyce's *Stephen Hero*, one does perceive that this is a remarkable passage for its psychological interest, suddenness of introduction, and complex imagery. There is a threatening tone in the hint of animism by which the stocks are "breathing heavily" and the syringa "on tiptoe," as if Mildred's bedroom were being invaded not by perfumes but by a strange man in the heat of passion. And as a curious complication, it is not these subtle images of sexual excitement but the lilies that keep Mildred awake. The "aching smell" of the lilies, usually associated with chastity, suggests that for her the very absence of sexual energy becomes a central bent, a predisposition to remain free and uncommitted which itself has the force of ordinary sensual excitement.

In the continuation of this passage Mildred goes on to speculate on the sex life of a couple she has just seen at a tennis party; she is puzzled because they seem to have so little in common (as in the early poem "The Hermaphrodite" it is the need to find a like image of oneself to love that provides the basis for Moore's image of the homosexual, an image little differentiated from simple lack of passion). For a person so little herself attracted to sex, Mildred spends a disproportionate amount of time thinking about it, perhaps because her approach to life is theoretical, uninvolved; "why should the idea transport and reality extinguish?" she wonders in the final chapter as she surveys her unsatisfactory life littered with precisely the untidy relationships she wanted to avoid.

Moore in *Modern Painting* had some hard things to say about women in art, suggesting that women succeed best in the home and the boudoir. For Mildred Lawson it is just the opposite. Attracted to art not because of her talent or will to achieve lasting work but rather because she admires the independence of ladies with their own studios, she decides to go to art school in Paris to elude her fiance, Ralph Hoskins. Even here Mildred is making another cardinal mistake from the point of view of *Modern Painting*, for Moore had argued there that the schools are destructive of individual talent with their tendency to inculcate standardized techniques and familiar ideas; her friend Ralph Hoskins, forced by poverty to remain in London, is driven back upon his own resources and becomes a fine and original artist. Once in Paris Mildred must choose between the men's studios and that of the ladies. Her decision to be with the men, despite the unruly atmosphere of their classes, is an admission that men have, indeed, achieved more in art, that to succeed in painting one must free oneself of the boudoir (but in a sense quite different from that intended by Moore, who felt that women writers dealing with essentially feminine matters, like Jane Austen, had done better than writers like George Eliot, who had masculinized themselves). At first Mildred does find the use of live models in the men's studios somewhat shocking, though characteristically she is more disturbed by undraped female than male models.

In a striking defense of her attendance at the men's studio Mildred makes the extraordinary claim, "there's no sex in art," thereby contriving to ignore not only a traditional subject for art (Mildred prefers to limit herself to landscapes, however) but also the numerous amours into which her fellow students are drawn in London and Paris. Mildred's statement by no very wonderful coincidence resembles the title of an article, "Sex in Art" from *Modern Painting*, to which allusion has already been made, and in fact constitutes an oversimplification of the argument expounded in that article. Moore makes the assertion in this little treatise that, contrary to received popular notions as expounded in innumerable novels, the artist does not devote a great deal of his time to the pursuit of love because his whole mind is given to his art. But Moore is speaking here exclusively of the male artist, the point being that man is by his nature ordinarily free of the preoccupations of the home and the boudoir. It is not necessary to comment now on this flawed but consistent reasoning, except to notice how Mildred departs from Moore's ideal by running off to join the men in their studio. (Mildred's assumption of a masculine identity has its effect on the other characters, too, because in a long comparison between himself, Mildred, and some ducks and drakes in St. James' Park, Ralph unconsciously assigns

Mildred the part of the drake.) And Mildred is unwilling to make the sacrifices to devote her whole mind to her art; hence her use of the argument is nothing but a case of special pleading, a peculiar form of selfishness.

Selfishness, in fact, is repeatedly named as a motive: Mildred tries to rationalize breaking off her engagement to Alfred Stanby by saying that all men are selfish; later she admits to Alfred in a comment remarkable for what it tells of her, "art may be only selfishness"; the socialist deputy Delacour scorns all private charity as selfishness. But when Mildred complains that her brother is selfish because he wants to keep her at home, Mrs. Fargus replies that all human beings are selfish, but that they only recognize selfishness when it takes a form different from their own. The rebuke is especially to the point because Mildred, with her inability to sympathize with other human beings, is particularly inclined to this vice, her various affairs being generally motivated by the simple desire to take away something desirable from someone else, just as she had as a child when she had wanted to win all the boys from the other girls. The aptly-named Alfred Stanby, who declares his willingness to wait twenty years, does not interest her; nor does Ralph Hoskins until she hears of his affair with Ellen Gibbs; and her coquetting with Morton Mitchell effectively takes him away from Rose Turner, his friend until the meeting with Mildred.

Seeing a painting by Greuse, she is drawn to it because its depiction of "the soul of a courtesan in the body of a virgin" so closely approximates her own state. Her strange desire not to marry but to have all the handsomest men in love with her accords with her purely theoretical experience of life, as does her transformation of real situations into imagined dramas in which she invariably plays the role of a heroine. Lacking any true passions, she perforce devises the outward show of sensuality without the substance. Naturally this leads to a certain duplicity. Converting to Catholicism because of its appeal to chastity, she sees nothing inconsistent about writing salacious society columns for *La Voix du Peuple*. It is as though there is no personal core which can be engaged in the transactions of life, no responsibility which may finally be assigned for the acts of cruelty or hypocrisy which, almost unconsciously, are issued during her career. No wonder that Morton Mitchell says she can never succeed in art because she is heartless (the motif endures: Mildred comes from a family with a history of weak hearts, her father and brother dying of heart attacks; she kills Ralph by breaking his heart; Alfred complains that his is breaking). As the story ends in a sleepless night which resembles that first night with which it opens, Mildred summarizes her life in a cry of agony: "(Give me a passion for God or man, but give me a passion. I cannot live without one)."

"Mildred Lawson" begins in the restless mind of its heroine, but "John Norton" opens with a description of Norton's mother. In the eight years that separated the first version of "John Norton" from the first version of "Mildred Lawson" Moore had become much less interested in the mysteries of atavism: the older story, "John Norton," is more concerned with family history and the disposition and character of parents. Mrs. Norton receives her guest, Parson Hare, with disapproval after his walk over the downs has made him too wet and muddy for her carpet; and over his helpless protests she sends him upstairs to find dry clothes. This scene evidences not only the maternal domination which has caused John to live away from home at Stanton College, but a foreshadowing in the parents of the disaster that is to overwhelm their children; for it is in crossing the downs much later that Kitty Hare suffers the rape and soiling of her clothes which causes her to run upstairs to hide in shame from her father.

But it is John Norton, after all, who is the central interest of this story; when at Mrs. Norton's bidding Mr. Hare goes to see John at his rooms in his Jesuit college, he finds a man full of contradictions in appearance, fleshy lips and earthy hands set against idealistic eyes, simple black clothes adorned with a rich, pearl pin. John is living at Stanton because of his chosen bachelorhood, feeling, the chagrinned Mrs. Norton reports, that "a woman might prove a disturbing influence in his life." The phrase relates not only to Mrs. Norton's most disturbing ways, but also to John's tendency to resist whatever is new or disturbing, and it unites his celibacy and his religious feeling as bulwarks against the changes of life.

Fanatically devout, still John is scarcely orthodox. He follows the pessimism of Schopenhauer to a point because he sees life as a series of desires demanding to be fulfilled, and consequently as a series of temptations concluded by dissatisfaction. His Christianity is that of the Latin Middle Ages, his heroes Augustine, Tertullian, and Marbodius (John quotes with approval Marbodius' poem that speaks of woman as a distraction and a temptress). He prefers to sit on unpadded furniture, suggests the maidservants attending Mass might prove a "temptation" to the boys, and, in a fit of comic asceticism, when he decides to leave Stanton, it is because he feels the priests are too worldly. In his appreciation for art, which is genuine, Norton differs again from his Jesuit hosts, who have adorned the college with imitation medieval furniture and imitation paintings, and who emphatically do not share his enthusiasm for the music of Wagner. Norton has sufficient esteem for Wagner to have travelled to Bayreuth to hear the master's operas performed, and speaks knowledgably of *Tristan und Isolde*, *The Ring*, and *Parsifal;* but it is with *Parsifal* he feels most comfortable, with its memories of the Middle Ages and the search for the Grail which he recalls with such nostalgia. Norton's creator, too, had great respect for the German musician, and as has been seen, made considerable use of Wagner's technique of structure through the employment of motif. Now this biographical fact is of some importance here, particularly when it is recalled that Moore acquired his taste for Wagner from his friend Dujardin, the editor of *La Revue Indépendante* and *La Revue Wagnérienne*. Moore accompanied Dujardin to see Paul Verlaine in order to arrange for the publication of that poet's short "Parsifal" in *La Revue Wagnérienne;* later he praised the same sonnet extravagantly in *Confessions of a Young Man*, saying that not even in Baudelaire or Poe can more perfect poetry be found. Verlaine's poem, which begins "Parsifal a vaincu les filles," makes Parsifal a rebel against the attractions of feminine charms, a fact which when coupled with Verlaine's well-known proclivities, has led many commentators to see the poem as homosexual in intent. The famous last line of the poem, "Et, ô ces voix d'enfants chantant dans la coupole!" becomes a structural motif in its own right in Moore's story. Norton at Bayreuth is chagrinned that the boys singing in the cupola have been replaced by women singers. Later, after a dream in which he sees Christ surrounded by a white million of youths, he meditates on Plato's theory of the origin of sexual preferences, his mind returning to the religious celebration of the Mass and the theme of salvation "held by a divine boy's voice for four bars high up in the cupola. . . ." The fusion of religious sentiment and sexual unorthodoxy in the poem also is characteristic of John Norton who sees himself in a vision of "ecstasy" when dreaming of his own ordination, who substitutes "the beautiful slim body" of Christ for his youthful temptations, who moves from a hatred of natural flesh to a worship of deified flesh.

Leaving Stanton, John decides to let the world be his monastery, a project he immediately interprets as renovating his ancestral home Thornby into a sort of abbey, to the loudly voiced consternation of his mother. But to his mother's delight and his own surprise, he is charmed by Kitty· Hare. Other girls displease him because of their obvious display of sexual maturity; Kitty attracts him because of the "boyish slightness" of her figure. Obviously, when put to the test such an attraction must evaporate, a consideration reinforced by the reflection that Mrs. Norton and Mr. Hare had also once felt for each other a kind of attraction which, however, was foiled by circumstances.

John Norton has spent most of his life in a sort of continuous repulsion of women. His friendship with Kitty Hare arouses in him first consternation, and then the recurrent fear that Kitty is a sort of temptress, overcoming his will. By the logic of Norton's association with the Parsifal role it inevitably follows that the temptress must be overcome by a man of violence (the ensuing events are not "a mere accident" at all, but the totally consequent effects of certain traits of character). Sitting with Kitty on the downs, John suddenly kisses her, with such violence and unexpectedness that she cries out; seeing that this kiss might be construed as a commitment, John hurriedly apologizes and hurries home, praying "that accident might lead him out of the difficulty." At that moment Kitty is raped on the downs by a stranger.

In many ways Kitty is almost as sexless a person as John. The shock of the rape sends her into a coma in which she has dreams which merge John's face with that of the rapist; when John comes to visit her, the anxiety to get away from him causes her to fall through the window. John after her funeral recognizes the kinship between his violent kiss and the violence that led to her death, but feels no sorrow, only horror at this image of his own baseness. Believing the whole episode to be a temptation from which he has been released, he sees it as evidence of the need for renunciation of the world and plans to turn Thornby Place into Thornby Abbey. This, of course, is precisely the wrong solution, since the fanatical hatred of life and sexuality is responsible for most of John's problems: like Mildred Lawson, John possesses a rudimentary sense of reality which leads him to misdiagnose his own problems, make false steps, become as ineffectual and impotent in art as he is in life.

The third story, "Agnes Lahens," is shorter than the other two, somewhat simpler, but also clearer in outline and intent. John Norton and Mildred Lawson had turned to religion because their inability to cope with the turbulence of life made them long for the changeless, passionless world implied by their beliefs. For Agnes Lahens the case is very slightly altered: she leaves the convent at the beginning of the story and is forced to come to terms with life. The novelist Harding a character in these stories, too, pondering the situation of this girl whose life in the convent has been so different from the promiscuities of her mother and her mother's friends, perceives a likeness between "the Faustines and the St. Theresas," the two extremes of existence which curiously resemble each other. For both, love is measured by suffering, whether it is a question of the lover deprived of his mistress, or the constant toil and hardship of the nun. Harding's formula works best perhaps for Major Lahens, a man who intensely dislikes his wife's amours, yet refuses to divorce her, living on ignominiously in his own house, a prisoner because of his very attachment to her. His room, "something like a monk's cell," small and unheated, is the place where he constantly types in order to raise the money for their support (which is not needed, due to his wife's wealth); his belief that one must earn money for self-respect is like the long toil of self-improvement which is the monk's sacrifice before he can deserve his God. But at times other people are drawn into Harding's equation. The young socialite Lilian Dare is told, for example, that to succeed in society she must leave her parent's home; even Mrs. Lahens, as she grows older, begins to hate the world she has worshipped in the days of her beauty, to hate it and to wish herself out of it. All this is very confusing for Agnes, of course, who inevitably returns to the convent she knows rather than remain in society, despite society's often surprising similarity to the convent. The convent at least is controlled and unchanging; Agnes returns there, seeing the rest of her life clearly fixed until her burial, the thought of which concludes the book.

When *Celibates* appeared in 1895 critics were generally not alive to its merits, nor indeed to its general features, often making unconvincing comparisons to Zola's work, or Stendhal's, or Thackeray's. A number of reviewers expressed the hope that the book not fall into the hands of young innocents, although there was nothing like the cry of dismay that had greeted Moore's rape story, "John Norton," on its first appearance in 1887 as *A Mere Accident*. Because of its density and imaginative use of image and motif, "John Norton" is perhaps the best of the stories in *Celibates;* but critics have generally preferred "Mildred Lawson," which is indisputably closer to Moore's personal preoccupations about life, marriage, and art. Henry Harland, after a perplexing attack on Moore's style, which he termed "almost classical," went on to praise "Mildred Lawson" as almost equal to Flaubert, were it not for Moore's inability to write.[10] With a few exceptions, very little has been said in favor of "Agnes Lahens," the slightest of the stories. Yet it is this story which was to be developed in *Evelyn Innes* and *Sister Teresa,* two long novels occupying the next six years of Moore's life.

CHAPTER 4

O To Be in Ireland

I Evelyn Innes

IN the concluding pages of *A Drama in Muslin* Moore had spoken of the decay of Dublin life as "the inevitable decay which must precede an outburst of national energy"; not many people were making this prediction in 1886, and it is doubtful that Moore expected the rebirth to come as soon as it did. But by 1894 Moore was listening to Edward Martyn (the original of John Norton) telling him of the founding of the Gaelic League in Ireland and of the interest in writing Irish literature in the Irish language. Moore was immediately enthusiastic. Had his articles on painting not thundered against the sapping dangers of cosmopolitanism and the need for art authentically related to its environment (that he had acquired these opinions from Dégas and Turgenev, a Frenchman and a Russian, bothered him not at all)? Besides, Moore had used Irish materials again and again in his novels; the opportunity to revisit his imaginative sources was a pleasing prospect which might well result in further novels.

Even in his years of absence from Ireland, Moore retained an interest in Irish matters and Irish writers. By 1893 he was telling his brother Maurice to treat cordially the then almost unknown W. B. Yeats, should he meet the poet in Dublin; in the same year he reviewed with praise Yeats's *The Celtic Twilight*; and by 1897 was proposing the joint collaboration on *Diarmuid and Grania*, the play which was to occupy so much time, involve so much controversy, and provide so much good copy for the recollections in *Hail and Farewell*. Gradually being drawn into operations of the Irish Literary Theatre, he worked closely, though not always amicably with Yeats, Edward Martyn, and Lady Gregory. In 1901 Moore installed himself in a house in Dublin. His reasons for this uprooting are not totally clear. The explanation offered at the time and repeated in *Hail and Farewell*, that his disgust with the Boer War made it impossible for him to live in England, would just as well explain a move to Paris. Perhaps one should accept at face value the remark in *A Communication to My Friends* that Moore went to seek an artistic rebirth in Ireland because he felt increasingly isolated and unappreciated as a literary figure in England. In any event, he did move to Dublin, lived there for ten years, and there he produced some of his finest works. The most distinctively Irish of the works between 1898 and 1911 are those written during Moore's actual residence in Dublin; but in all the books of this period can be detected, sometimes indirectly, the preoccupations and enthusiasms of his involvement in Irish affairs.

It had been a long time since Moore had taken notes for the writing of *A Mummer's Wife*, but even at this post-naturalist stage he was not above doing some research: for his new novel he consulted the opera singer Melba and Arthur Symons on music, its performance and interpretation; and he used his friend Mrs. Virginia Crawford as a go-between to supply him with information on convent life. No wonder the novel sometimes seems as airless, involved, and ponderous as if it were an opera itself ("too much brass in the orchestra," remarked Moore thirty years later); it is as if the libretto were too rich and complicated to permit a satisfactory musical setting. Moore himself had difficulty describing exactly what he was up to in *Evelyn Innes*, telling his brother in April of 1898 that it was worse than Balzac and Turgenev, better than "trashy Thackeray and rubbishy Dickens and pompous Eliot"; that it could not be judged anyway until the appearance of its sequel, *Sister Teresa*; finally, that it was difficult to do anything new in literature because Shakespeare had appropriated dramatic poetry, Wagner dramatic music, and Balzac the novel. He did not tell his brother at this time of his incorporation of operatic material, nor of convent life, nor of his discussions with Arnold Dolmetsch about archaic instruments, nor of his use of mythology. *Evelyn Innes* and *Sister Teresa* constitute, in scope at least, the most ambitious and complex work of Moore's life, a work that in intention, though not in anything like the same degree of artistic success, might well be ranked with Joyce's *Ulysses*.

The story opens with Mr. Innes, the man one would judge the least important of the central characters. Yet in his past he has had a

life with some relevance to that of his daughter Evelyn, for he has
given up the temptation of a public career as an organist in order to
devote himself to a revival of Palestrina and the old music, a choice
which has brought him into opposition with the incurably bad taste
of the priests. He marries an opera singer with a voice as fine as that
destined to be inherited by Evelyn; this lady's European celebrity is
broken suddenly by the loss of her voice in Brussels. Her death,
three years before the events of the novel take place, leaves the
Innes family dependent on the father's church engagements and the
daughter's lessons under conditions which make it unlikely that
Evelyn will ever be able to afford proper voice teachers. In this
account is implicit a great deal of the action of the book, beyond
Evelyn's obvious predisposition toward anyone who can give her the
chance to develop her singing abilities. Her mother's mysterious
withdrawal from the operatic pursuits that have brought so much
fame, her father's rejection of a career as a successful public per-
former, the unformulated but unmistakable opposition between religion and art—all these elements are to be recombined in the
course of Evelyn's life, and already constitute the essential features
of that life.

But this background, while suggestive of things to come, is not
causal in any genetic or simplistically environmental sense, because
experience here does not have the hard-edged and distinctively
featured complexion of physical law. On the contrary, it is elusive
and profoundly unpredictable: "Our lives are enveloped in mystery,
the scientist concedes that, and the woof of which the stuff of life is
woven is shot through with many a thread of unknown origin, un-
traceable to any earthly shuttle. There is a mystery, and in the
elucidation of that mystery man never tires. . . . " Consequently
one's encounters are mysterious, mentalized, internalized; at first
sight of Owen Asher, Evelyn is conscious not of the famous embroidered waistcoat and gold cuff-links, but of the "completely unknown," which yet she seems always to have carried in her heart.
Apart from Evelyn, the characters in the novel seem to represent
ideas, possible choices which she might make, rather than exter-
nally existing entities. Hence the two great choices of Evelyn's life
are present at this same first concert: Asher with his dash, arro-
gance, and splendid appearance, Ulick Dean with his poetry,
"priest's profile," and clumsy boots. Again, much of the narrative is
occupied by events that are purely mental in nature, dreams or

reflections which themselves mirror the various scenes they introduce or conclude; and at any given time it is difficult to be certain
that these mental events are not more important than their counterparts in the public transactions of the novel.

Allured by the prospect of giving a great opera singer to the world
and, incidentally, an attractive mistress to himself, Owen encourages Evelyn to leave for the Continent with him. In making this
offer, Asher is offering a crucial choice not only to Evelyn but to
himself, for hitherto his affairs have been transient, without risk,
capricious. He sees Evelyn as the last chance for a great love adventure in life, but at the same time an unprecedented gamble, since it
is at least possible that her voice will never fulfill its promise and
that he will have given his remaining years of youth to a pretty
mediocrity. His tendency to call her "Eve," as will be seen, is an
indication of the temptation, the peculiar invitation to a new mode
of existence, that he finds in Evelyn Innes. But despite the scruples
of conscience which are never to desert her, Evelyn does accept
Asher's invitation, does become his mistress (and for all her in-
quietude of conscience, she becomes an agnostic for most of the
time she lives with Owen: her choice of companion is associated
with a choice of beliefs)—and she does, in time, become a celebrated singer. Unfortunately, Owen represents only one side of life,
the materialistic side, as defined by his gold cuff-links and gold
moustache and his tendency to find simplistic, physical explanations
for the dreams in which Evelyn sets so much stock. One night,
preparing to play in Wagner's opera, *Tristan und Isolde*, she has still
another dream in which she is Isolde, but there are two Tristans, the
dark and the fair, between whom she must choose: her unconscious
deformation of the opera is a simple mistake, but it signals the great
change that is to take place as she chooses between the fairhaired Sir
Owen Asher and the dark Ulick Dean.

If Asher symbolizes the material world, Ulick Dean just as
strongly represents the spiritual and intuitive side of life. Ulick
plainly, with his lock of hair falling over his forehead, the priestly
profile, and the general Celtic air, is meant to be a depiction of
William Butler Yeats as given in J. B. Yeats's famous portrait. Moore
often included overt or covert descriptions of his acquaintances in
his work; but there is in this identification a significance not to be
found, for example in Asher's resemblance to Sir William Eden. The
year before *Evelyn Innes* appeared, Moore had begun his collabora-

tion with William Butler Yeats on the play *Diarmuid and Grania*, and thus presented himself as a champion of the Celtic Revival; this was a change in direction for the ex-boulevardier comparable to those made by Evelyn Innes. Now the character Ulick Dean is working on an opera, for which he has chosen the name *Grania*, and which covers the same ground as that to be traversed by the Moore-Yeats play. Essentially Grania in the play is the same sort of person as Evelyn, a mixture of strength, fickleness, and impetuosity, constantly refusing definition and a puzzlement to her friends. Grania, like Evelyn, is forced to make a choice between an older man and a younger, Finn and Diarmuid, the play itself being the record of this decision. Both the play and the novel end somewhat indecisively, *Diarmuid and Grania* after Diarmuid's death but before a reconciliation with Finn, *Evelyn Innes* with Evelyn meditating on life in the convent but unsure that she will not return to Asher. Further, the comparison between the materialistic Asher and the sun, in numerous references (while Dean is constantly described in terms of darkness, the moon or stars), exactly duplicates the use of the symbols of the solar and lunar phases to imply objective and subjective life in Yeats's *A Vision* and many of his poems from his earliest career onwards. After his quarrel with Yeats in 1901, Moore rewrote the novel, assigning Ulick's role to a tall bearded figure with the same name and an uncanny resemblance to George (AE) Russell. It is not an improvement.

In love with two men at one time, and consequently in a sort of neutralized zone of influence, Evelyn becomes more and more subject to her conscience, responsive again to the life she had lived at Dulwich before the appearance of Owen Asher. She becomes less interested in singing opera, less obviously sensual, and more religious, following a law which has controlled her all along ("it was sex that made her an artist"). Unlike Owen Asher and Ulick Dean, who in their various ways face the problem of how life might be lived most intensely, nuns yield the present, a thought fascinating to Evelyn, who is always concerned about the future. As she gives up her music and her life of sensuality, it is natural in a sense that she should be drawn to convent life, with its absolute concentration on the future, its changelessness, and even its lack of art. Nuns appear and reappear throughout the novel, in Dulwich, in Florence, in Wimbledon, always associated with that carelessness of the present and its toil which offers a permanent imaginative oasis to Evelyn's turbulent life (an anecdote which offers an amusing confirmation of this principle is found in the convent gardener who converts to Catholicism and henceforth disregards his work). At the close of the narrative Evelyn has completed the transition from Faustine to St. Theresa, the two related opposite limits of human life described by Harding in *Celibates*. But her decision for religious life is tentative and speculative in *Evelyn Innes*; for the story of her existence in the cloister the reader must turn to *Sister Teresa*.

By Victorian standards *Evelyn Innes* does not have a very complicated plot, but by any standards the novel is nevertheless enormously involved in its narrative texture and characterization. Long fascinated by the success of Wagner, who constructed complex and cathedral-like edifices using the simplest materials, by the introduction and combination of motifs, Moore set out not only to create a heroine who sings Wagner, but a Wagnerian novel. Some of Moore's motifs he took directly from Wagner, such as the comparisons between Evelyn and Tannhaüser, both of whom are faced with a choice between sensuality and penitence. Wagner is used again in the invocation of Tristan and Isolde, those lovers doomed by fate to the curse of fickleness. It is possible that Moore knew through Yeats that the Diarmuid and Grania legend is one of the sources of the Tristan and Isolde story; almost certainly Yeats first recounted the legend to Moore, who in few other places shows knowledge of or interest in Irish mythology. Whatever the truth of this particular matter, Moore did use the legend to considerable effect, as has been seen, and the association of Ulick Dean with Diarmuid is of great importance to the novel.

Owen Asher customarily calls Evelyn "Eve" or "Evie." To this seemingly innocuous contraction are attached many narrative threads: the two scenes in the garden under the tree where Evelyn speaks of love first to Owen and, much later, to Ulick; the snake Evelyn refuses to kill after she falls in love with Ulick; the sacrifice which Owen is obliged to make for his love. But there are many other patterns overlaying the narrative which have relevance to Evelyn—Balzac's Honorine; Ulick's other opera, *Connla and the Fairy Woman*, about another temptress; even the Medusa (the name of Asher's yacht). These parallel narratives, too complex and diffused throughout the text to be discussed fully here, make of the novel something much more than a simple tale. It is rather a tapestry, a mosaic. (Both these words have been used to describe Joyce's procedure in *Ulysses*, a book technically very like *Evelyn Innes*. William Blissett has provided an interesting commentary on the use of Wagnerism by Moore and Joyce.)[1] For a novelist writing in 1898 *Evelyn Innes* is a prophetic and innovative work, of permanent interest for the literary historian, and still capable of considerable power for the contemporary reader.

Writers of prophetic or innovative books are often misunderstood. As ever, Moore expected a critical success with this latest work. Compared with the scorn cast on some of his work, *Evelyn Innes* escaped lightly, but its author was stung almost into believing he had spent three years of his life on "the invention of an imbecility." Although some reviewers were still hunting grimly for unacceptable traces of Naturalism, most divided their comments between praise of the psychological sureness of the book and condemnation of its clogged style. One reviewer delivered himself of the fatal observation that Moore was a fine critic and had better stick to that, rather than writing such unclear fiction in such woeful prose: this was a criticism made several times in his career, and Moore was generally enraged by it. None saw, perhaps could not be expected to see, that the style of the novel was clogged with detail precisely because of the experiments with melodic detailing which constituted Moore's adaptation of Wagnerian motifs. In any event, the new style does often show lapses of taste, some of which survived through several editions, as well as occasional solecisms of another nature. The gift of "almost thoroughbred" horses from Sir Owen Asher to Evelyn and the brown boots which Owen wears in society at noon caused Oscar Wilde to make his famous remark that George Moore conducted his education in public, a comment which prompted Robert Ross's rejoinder that since the book-buying public were paying for that education they had a right to know how Moore was getting on.[2]

II Sister Teresa

In *Celibates*, *A Mere Accident*, and *Mike Fletcher* Moore had depicted sympathetically people seeking religion as an alternative to existence embroiled in the upsets of the world; but in writing *Sister Teresa* he may have come upon an uncongenial subject. Convent life is not remarkable for its variety—indeed this is partly the basis of Evelyn's decision—and two hundred and thirty pages of convent life have proved tedious for too many readers. In the preface the

novelist claims that *Evelyn Innes* and *Sister Teresa* were in conception one novel, but that as work progressed his publisher took alarm
and proposed a division into two novels. If this is a true account, it
does explain why *Evelyn Innes* is a much denser novel than *Sister
Teresa*, which covers very little new ground in terms of psychological motivation or the philosophical alternatives proposed. A further
difficulty for the reader is that the first edition of *Sister Teresa* is not
in direct sequence to the first edition of *Evelyn Innes*, but to the
revised second edition, from which Moore eliminated many of the
distinctive stylistic features of the original and which consequently
is quite different in tone. If the first edition of *Evelyn Innes* was
made too rich by its narrative overlays, the first edition of its sequel,
already almost insubstantial in plot, is impoverished by its comparative simplicity. But this is perhaps an overstatement. Much common ground is shared by the two books; enough, for example, to
make it necessary to have read the first to understand Ulick's comment in the second that only Evelyn can properly sing the role of his
Grania. More importantly, Evelyn's mysterious choices in *Sister
Teresa*, particularly her choice to remain in the convent at the end,
are only explicable by the laws of her personality as developed in
Evelyn Innes.

Partly because of its separation from the narrative intricacy of
Evelyn Innes, partly from an authentic bias of its own, *Sister Teresa*
is an even more indefatigably mentalized novel than its predecessor,
as these opening lines strongly indicate:

She was conscious of her indolence: within and without her there was a
strange, lifeless calm, a strange inactivity in the air and in her mind. In the
landscape and in her there seemed no before and no hereafter. But a glance
inwards revealed to her the ripple of some hidden anticipation stirring
under the surface. The idea of returning to London stirred a little dread in
her, yet she felt that for the moment she had seen enough of the convent.
For the moment she could assimilate no more of it. The rhythm of the
carriage penetrated her indolent body. The thud of the chestnuts' hoofs in
the empty road stirred a quiet wonder in her, and she looked into the sunset
as she might into a veil.

Here the object of attention is not action, not thoughts of action, but
consciousness itself, as defined by the investigation of two almost
conflicting levels of awareness, the mental state of inactivity and the
more remote mental state which is not quite satisfied with inactiv-

ity. Moreover, consciousness is not clearly made distinct from the material envelope of life: Evelyn seems to locate much of her awareness in the landscape around her; and the wonder she feels is somehow provoked by the thud of the horses' hooves by a process in which consciousness seems to contain her experiences. (Moore was to use this technique again in *The Lake*, which has a quite similar opening passage, and which also associates the subtle operations of the mind with rippling water.) Yet there will be many times in Evelyn's career when she will be unable to attain this level of meditation, for she resembles Esther Waters and Kate Ede in that her moments of lucidity and moments of decision and action rarely come together. This reverie, made hypnotic by its rhythmic cycling and repetitions of words like "indolence," "strange," and "stirred," reveals an uncharacteristic poise in a life scarcely capable of understanding itself for long periods of time.

Other, more local, features of this moment of consciousness merit comment. Evelyn has just left her retreat in the convent, and consequently her mind is saturated with details which (for Moore anyway) relate to religious life. The act of looking into a veil is not an act of so distinct a kind that it can helpfully be used to explain a certain way of looking into a sunset: only by emphasizing the veil as a religious symbol can any point be given to the final statement. That this is so is, in any event, confirmed by the employment of the motif elsewhere. Of course, sunset, particularly in view of Owen Asher's association with the sun in *Evelyn Innes*, is an especially appropriate circumstance here, since this is the point at which Evelyn is ready to renounce her attachment to Owen. Evelyn's inclination to indolence is also to be related to her conversion ("religion always seems to fling me into a waste of idleness," she complains in another context) because the emphasis upon waiting for the consummation of life after death implies a disregard for temporal affairs. This is tantamount to saying that religion is, on a certain level, no more than a death wish, a notion already found in *Celibates* and *A Drama in Muslin* and here reinforced by the words "lifeless," "calm," and "inactivity."

When Evelyn enters the convent as Sister Teresa, the rule that her art is incompatible with religious life generated in *Evelyn Innes* disposes her to think that she is finished forever with her singing. But the Mother Superior has quite a different point of view; for she inclines to regard Evelyn not only as a fashionable penitent of the sort which her order has often attracted, but also as a kind of financial windfall sent providentially to attract the donations of rich Catholics by her voice. Evelyn naturally does follow the suggestions of the Prioress, but her nature is forced in a direction totally at variance with her vocation; and she becomes almost as agnostic as she had in her career with Owen. This current of dissatisfaction becomes more and more pronounced until the final chapter, when her friend Louise Heilbron finds Evelyn unaccountably resigned and at peace in her life. As an apparent aside in response to Louise's questions, Evelyn provides what is, in fact, the explanation of her new condition: "I lost my voice last winter; a heavy cold took it all away. . . ."

As a general rule, critics who had not liked *Evelyn Innes* did not care for *Sister Teresa* either, though not necessarily for the same reasons. *Evelyn* had been caviar to the general with its elaborate effects; but now reviewers were concerned about what they detected as monotony in the simpler scheme of *Sister Teresa*. Very few tried to beat Moore with the stick of Naturalism, though in his comparisons to Huysmans, Harry Thurston Peck made Moore a post-Naturalist (and not inappropriately: several of the blasphemous dream sequences from *Sister Teresa* do seem to owe something to *Là-Bas*).[3] Curiously, Huysmans, hearing that Moore was at work on a novel of convent life, had said that the subject was an unpromising one, an opinion which many readers later shared. From a much longer perspective than that possible to the reviewers of 1901, *Sister Teresa*, whether viewed as the second half of a very long novel or a novel in its own right, survives mainly as a curiosity, a transition piece, rather than as one of Moore's strongest or most durable productions. In retrospect it seems a failure, though a failure of the kind only a very fine novelist could write.

III   The Untilled Field

A memoirist who is also a distinguished practitioner of fiction perhaps may be forgiven when his recollections are marked by the finish of art rather than the untidy irregularity of truth. In the preface to the 1903 Tauchnitz edition, addressed to John Eglinton, this famous statement is made:

As we walked through Rathmines I told you a little story about an Irish dancing-girl, and you suggested that I should write a volume of stories about Irish life which would be, you said, a book of memories vivified by the independent observation and criticism of one returning to his native country. You said, I think, that I should take Tourgenieff's *Tales of a Sportsman* as model. My heart failed me, and I think I answered that it were as well to ask me to paint like Corot.

That Eglinton did make this suggestion is certain, for he has confirmed it; what is not so certain is that *The Untilled Field* grew from this suggestion. Of the thirteen stories in the first English edition of 1903, three had been published in an earlier form between 1887 and 1893, and hence date from a period prior to Moore's acquaintance with Eglinton. Since most of the stories were written or rewritten in 1901 and 1902, possibly Moore was trying to recast the older stories into the mold of the newer ones, in accordance with Eglinton's advice, but it is remarkable that the otherwise helpful and abundant correspondence with his publisher does not make this comparison at the time. Actually the stories are not stylistically of a piece, and some of them are decidedly unlike Turgenev. Probably what excited Moore in Eglinton's recommendation was the association between Turgenev and the delineation of the soul of a country, for in his 1888 article on the Russian novelist, he had this to say about *Fathers and Sons:* "Who among the many who have thought of turning the troubles of Ireland to literary account has not thought of an Irish Bazaroff. . . ." The "troubles of Ireland" are, of course, the civil disturbances of the 1880s, a subject Moore had turned into a book of short stories, *Parnell and his Island*, in 1887, a book much closer in tone to Turgenev than *The Untilled Field.*

It has been suggested that the title of Moore's novel is taken from that of Turgenev's *Virgin Soil.* [4] This seems doubtful as an attribution, not only because Moore's title is not persuasively close to Turgenev's, but also because his boyhood memories of Shelley would have probably made him aware of the often anthologized sonnet "England in 1819" with its remarkably apposite line, "A people starved and stabbed in the untilled field." Now this does not prove that Moore was uninfluenced by Turgenev: his criticism and, more importantly, his practice, from the late 1880s onwards shows a constant, though perhaps diffused, debt to the Russian writer. It does seem plain, however, that Moore did not compose the stories of *The Untilled Field* with this specific and unvarying model before him. His letters of the time show that although he was determined that the unity of the book be observed, he was always changing his mind as to what it was that gave the book its unity. Turgenev became a convenient point of reference; and Moore thankfully accepted Eglinton's suggestion as a useful fiction.

In the original Gaelic version of *The Untilled Field* two stories, "In the Clay" and "The Way Back," had not yet been written, and in all subsequent revisions after the first English edition they were eliminated from the collection. This is a pity because "In the Clay" in particular is a very fine story, equal to any in the book, and one laments the principle of selection that led to its elimination. By 1902 when these stories were written, Moore had become cautious in his enthusiasm for the Celtic Revival, inclined to qualify his hopes by expressing the need to counter the excessive clerical influence which he considered harmful to art. Later he became totally cynical that any real regeneration was possible in Ireland, and his pruning of these stories, which more than any others represent the equilibrium of his opinions of 1902, conforms to his subsequent frame of mind.

John Rodney of "In the Clay" is the son of a Dublin builder, whose expressed wish, even before his son is born, is to be the father of a sculptor. Moore in *Modern Painting* had said that the gift of the artist is incommunicable, that it is the product of a unique sensibility, so there is perhaps in this transmitted vocation already an implied criticism. Again in *Modern Painting* Moore railed especially against two things, art schools and cosmopolitanism; but John is something of a champion student, attending art schools in Dublin and Paris. When he seeks work, it is not in Dublin until driven home by want of money, but first in England and Scotland where he works for other sculptors. This hero of "In the Clay" is already condemned by the standards of *Modern Painting* as too cosmopolitan, too educated in the ways of art schools, too prone to look to the inspiration of the past rather than to investigate his own vision in the present. His complaint that good work cannot be done in Ireland because "sculpture is native to the orange zone," is a sort of evasion of the duty of the artist to communicate what is "racy of the soil," to use a phrase frequently employed by Moore.

These observations about the artistic limitations of John Rodney are necessary because he is so persuasive about the shortcomings of Ireland as a place for art; it is important to realize that he is representing a partial view when he speaks as follows of his native land:

"This is no place for a sculptor to live in. It is no country for an educated man. It won't be fit for a man to live in for another hundred years. It is an unwashed country, that is what it is!" Rodney, in fact, voices the opinions of the George Moore of 1887, the George Moore who had angered landlords and patriots alike with his suggestion that Ireland was not only barbarous but retrograde in the fierce criticisms of *Parnell and his Island*. Against Rodney is balanced the milder view of the novelist Harding: "Harding believed, or was inclined to believe, that the Gael was not destined to disappear, that in making the Cross of Cong he had not got as far as he was intended to get. But even Harding had admitted that no race had taken to religion quite so seriously as the Celt." Only a question of emphasis really separates these views, for Harding can see as well as Rodney the defects of a country controlled by a grossly clerical mentality; his inclination to hope is based rather on expectations of an unfathomable future than on the realities of a dismal present. Harding here voices the sanguine views of the George Moore of 1902, views destined for a definitive revision within a few months of the writing of this story.

One day Rodney goes to his studio to find the clay model of a Virgin and Child destroyed. He is overcome because he had hoped to use the money from this religious commission to leave Ireland forever; doubly so in that he has been told that this is his best work. Harding had advised him not to put draperies on the nude group, a perfectly "pagan" bit of work, but Rodney's plan was to put a conventional head on the piece and sell it to the cathedral as a Madonna in order to secure the money from the commission. His compromise, understandable from a financial point of view, is a violation of his opinion that there is no such thing as religious sculpture, that art is either folklore or paganism (Moore's very similar comments in *Modern Painting*), and one further proof of his inadequacies as an artist.

Rodney had found a model to sit for the portrait, a girl named Lucy who worked as a typist. Rodney at length succeeded in satisfying her scruples about sitting in the nude for a religious sculpture, but not those of Father McCabe, who was unaware that even religious subjects require nude models. Father McCabe's scandalized comments to Lucy's parents lead not only to a heated family discussion but to the destruction of the statue by Lucy's brothers; hence in a sense Rodney is right when he finds the ruins of his clay group and says that the priests must have done it. The vandalism of which Rodney is a victim is a special application of the general law that makes religion and art incompatible, particularly in Ireland, where religion has so strong and unshakable a hold.

Religion and art are visualized almost as competing vocations in "In the Clay" from the day that John as a youth refuses to go to Mass, and his father excuses that decision on the ground that no one can do two things at once, and that John has decided to do sculpture. The "love and veneration" that John puts into the statue is a mark of his "vocation," a vocation unfortunately undertaken at some risk in Ireland, which has put all its intelligence into religion since the sixth century. Rodney's complaint against the priests is that "they blaspheme against life," a curiously ecclesiastical charge with regard to choice of words: the image is taken up again in connection with the sculpture, which John Rodney thinks of "as one thinks of a corpse," or which makes him believe "that the living have turned to clay." That religion is a special sort of death-wish is a notion familiar to readers of Moore from A Drama in Muslin onwards. One can judge from this how measured the novelist's optimism must be when he seeks an artistic renaissance in a country that must have a religious revolution before that renaissance takes place.

The companion story to "In the Clay," which completes the framing effect by ending the book just as "In the Clay" has begun it, is "The Way Back." Harding and Rodney meet one day in London, Rodney about to leave for the yellowing marbles of Italy, Harding, to Rodney's astonishment, on the point of moving to Dublin. Harding's decision is unshakable and yet strangely inaccessible: he begins by speaking of the ugliness of London, a new ability to perceive the beauty of Ireland, his desire to find out what Paddy Durkin and Father Pat will say. None of this is of much value as a coherent argument; indeed Harding says that everyone regards him as mad. What seems primary is an almost mystical sense of the necessity for him to make this return to his own land: "I felt I should like to live among these people again. There is a proverb in Irish which says that no man ever wanders far from his grave sod. We are thrown out, and we circle a while in the air, and return to the feet of the thrower." All this is in perfect accord with a number of Moore's views on art, as has been seen, but the narrative presents the views not with the cogency of a critical opinion but with the fluid tentativeness of a biographical whim. Harding, now in his forties, a novelist of reputation with a considerable amount of time spent in France behind him, is very clearly George Moore at the time of his return to Ireland, excited at the prospects which the new movement opens for him, anxious to find new sources and new methods, yet not quite sure, when the time has come, that he is not perhaps making a fool of himself.

"Some Parishioners," the second tale in the collection, is very long—so long, in fact, that it was successfully divided into several shorter tales in subsequent editions. Ulick Dean had lamented in *Sister Teresa* that Evelyn Innes, in choosing Catholicism, was choosing the most materialistic of all spiritual disciplines; "Some Parishioners" is a story devoted to the interpenetration of religious motive and material fact, and as such is the most humane in sympathy and most filled with smiling indulgence of all the stories. The basis of the story is a sly analogy between the idealistic but censorious Father Maguire, and his obstinate yet shrewd parishioner Biddy M'Hale. Father Maguire and Biddy obviously regard each other as adversaries, for his determination to raise money for a new church is constantly thwarted by her obstinate wish to give her money for a new window without using any for the construction of the church. As their architectural ambitions indicate, they exist in a reciprocal relationship. Father Maguire's comment about Biddy's mania for the window, "It is extraordinary . . . how a desire for immortality possesses these second-class souls," could equally well apply to his obsession with a new building. He thinks of her as grasping, interested less in spiritual matters than in her own glorification, but his own habitual thoughts are filled with comparisons of virtues to money in the bank. At one point he even refuses to marry Mary Byrne and Ned Kavanaugh because Ned can only produce two pounds, instead of the five pounds Maguire needs for the church. When, as a result, Ned and Mary contrive the marriage without the wedding, Maguire is duly penitent, but as unenlightened as before that his own tendency to reduce spiritual matters to cold cash is the reason for the disarray.

No one with the habitual inclination to meddle in worldly matters possessed by Father Maguire could ever be quite so naive as he about the nexus between the temporal and the eternal. When the Salvation Army invades his parish in step to the inevitable music, Maguire, scenting "heresy," creates a scandal by cutting the skin of a drum with a carving knife, an act which draws the criticism of his

own Vicar General. This foolishness continues: he "makes" the marriage of Ned Kavanaugh and Mary Byrne, with the results already
described; he attempts again to "make" another marriage, that of
Peter M'Shane and Kate Kavanaugh, but the marriage evaporates
on the wedding night and Kate leaves for America. At a lecture
organized at the schoolhouse, the scheduled speaker on poultry
does not arrive; promptly Maguire delegates a newcomer to the
parish to give the talk, even though she knows nothing of the subject
and although some in the audience know a great deal, Maguire's
rationale being that the book the lady carries must be "full of instruction." Like Father Maguire's beloved textbooks of St. Thomas
Aquinas, the speaker's book (of what kind one is never informed) is
unequal to the practical application set before it, and the audience
begins to smile. Prominent among the smilers is Biddy M'Hale,
whose moderate wealth has come from raising chickens. On this
level she is aware of Father Maguire's comical excesses, just as he is
of hers when it comes to the question of the window; as politely as
she can, she explains that although in theory it is a good idea to
bring chickens to market in January, as a practical matter it is quite
impossible.

Biddy's sound common sense at this stage merits remark, because
later, under the influence of the religious mania associated with the
stained-glass window, she becomes truly alienated, allowing her
chickens to die and becoming reduced to life in an outhouse,
nourished by bits of bread and potatoes. But she has her window, a
window she describes for a stranger with comical enthusiasm:

At the top of the picture, where the window narrowed to a point, Our Lord
sat dressed in white upon a throne, placing a golden crown on the head of
the virgin kneeling before him. About him were gathered the women who
had loved him, and the old woman said she was sorry she was not a nun, and
hoped that Christ would not think less of her. As far as mortal sin was
concerned she could say she had never committed one. At the bottom of the
window were suffering souls. The cauldrons that Biddy wished to see them
in, the agent said, would be difficult to introduce—the suffering of the souls
could be artistically indicated by flames.

Father Stafford, the Vicar General, makes the acute comment in
one episode that all of Father Maguire's difficulties arise because his
own celibacy imposes too narrow a limit to his perceptions of life.
Biddy also is perforce a celibate, her hunchbacked condition caused

by a fall downstairs; the strongly autobiographical element in her window, in which Christ is surrounded by the Virgin Mary and the women he loved, is a compensation for the lack of love in her own life, and an explanation of the emotional energy which Biddy is able to absorb from the picture, even to the point of wearing the blue gown of the Virgin to church. The absurd juxtaposition of the souls of the blessed and their unfortunate brethren in agony (a detail Moore borrowed from Villon) is grotesquely simplistic, but the simplicity is kin to the severity of Father Maguire, who would gladly slit a drum for Christ's sake. Biddy's case progresses to the point of plain insanity. Still the progression is logical enough: as Father Maguire observes, she has abandoned the things of the world, only to replace them with the realities she finds in the window: and in so doing she has reached a condition not unlike the conventional idea of sanctity. To Maguire's chagrin this local "saint" attracts a great deal of attention, and it is only through Biddy that he is able to raise sufficient money to complete his church. But this is more than a paradox. Before Biddy's demented moment of grace, "her faith in her money was abundant"; later her association with the five-pound-priest, Father Maguire, leads not only to her own spiritual celebrity, but to a good, solid church with lath and plaster walls and the most prosperous-looking saints' statues for many miles around.

In "The Exile" there is a development of the theme indicated by Rodney's bitter observation in "In the Clay" that nothing flourishes in Ireland except the religious vocation: Peter Phelan is attracted to the priesthood, partly because of his vision of the material comfort of the priest, who has the only arm chair in the village, partly because of his own inability to cope with the simple demands of farm life, partly because he does not want to take Catherine Ford from his brother James. But when Peter enters the seminary, Catherine becomes a nun, leaving James wretchedly unhappy in the contemplation of this derisory triangle. Peter, feckless as ever, is unable to persevere; he returns home to the farm he does not particularly like and marries Catherine after all, despite his own want of inclination to her or to marriage. James emigrates to America, becoming an exile. But Peter, tied down to a life he does not relish, is also a sort of exile, as is Catherine, married to a loveless husband. This cheerless prospect, of the best men going to America, leaving the pious, the unhappy, and the unable behind, is that announced by John Rodney in the first story: "Ireland is emptying before them . . .

They blaspheme against Life . . . My God, what a vile thing is the
religious mind." Moore had enough firsthand knowledge of the conditions of the 1870s and 1880s to know of the material reasons for
Irish emigration; but here he views these material reasons as far less
important than the aboriginal hatred of life produced by generations
of Catholicism. Exile is almost a mystical word of release for James
Phelan, for John Rodney, for all the active human beings depicted in
The Untilled Field, who choose this way of asserting their freedom
not from the limitations of poverty, climate, and opportunity, but
from a far more powerful and ubiquitous limitation of spirit.

Father MacTurnan of "A Letter to Rome" is the most humane of
the priests depicted in *The Untilled Field*, the most humane and yet
the most limited, the most humorously maladroit of all. Moved by
the case of James Murdoch, who may not marry Catherine Mulhare
until he earns the price of a pig, MacTurnan thinks of the comfortable life of the clergy, who alone can afford to marry, but who are
debarred from marriage by their pledged celibacy. His solution is
not to complain of the disproportion by which those who need the
income to support a family are deprived by those without such a
need, but to urge marriage for priests in order to prevent Ireland's
inevitable depopulation from making it a Protestant country. Just as
John Norton in *Mike Fletcher* is betrayed into absurdities by the
requirements of a religion at variance with his own nature, Father
MacTurnan fuzzily translates his own real sympathies for the plight
of people like James Murdoch into the naive project of writing to
Rome to ask the Pope to absolve Ireland of the obligation of priestly
celibacy.

MacTurnan's letter is received in Rome and read with interest,
although not by the Pope: a note from a papal secretary about these
doubtful opinions is dispatched, and in due time a summons is
issued from the bishop's palace. Tired from walking fifteen miles,
Father MacTurnan arrives late, but is nevertheless told that the
bishop wants to see him immediately; for the first time a peculiar
manner in the bishop's assistant gives him cause to doubt that
perhaps the Pope may not place the Irish clergy on the same footing
as their Greek brethren, but he prepares to explain himself as well
as he can. As soon as the bishop has satisfied himself that his subor-
dinate has not become involved in some scandalous liaison for which
his letter is only a sort of covering rationale (and after MacTurnan, in
confusion, has declared his near-aversion to marriage and to
women), the story of James Murdoch is related together with Mac-

Turnan's reasons for Church reform. The bishop is shrewd enough
to penetrate to the essential part of this analysis: he offers five
pounds for James Murdoch to buy a pig, and the priest leaves without a further thought of his scheme to prevent the depopulation of
Ireland.

MacTurnan is a comical figure, to be sure, but he is important
because, like Rodney, he just fails to put his finger on the right spot
on the map. After all, Moore himself saw a celibate clergy as a
severe impediment to progress in Ireland; indeed some of MacTurnan's comments could have been made without alteration by his
creator speaking in his own voice, as in this remark: "Religion, like
everything else, must be national . . . . Religion, like art, came
from the parishes." MacTurnan's argument that religion in Ireland
should have a local, not a cosmopolitan form, may in fact be the
program for "working with the priests" that Moore held up as an
ideal when he first returned to Ireland but never clearly enunciated.
This notion, that the present religious condition of Ireland was ines-
sential, corrigible, may have given hope to the convert of 1901 and
1902; yet, once again, MacTurnan's failure demonstrates how uncertain and tentative those hopes were.

In the short story "Julia Cahill's Curse" there are not one but two
priests, the progressive and admirable Father O'Hara, and the severe and repressive Father Madden; but the narrator prefers to
speak of Madden because, as he says, one finds stories in the lives of
the weak and the improvident. Madden has "put down" the ball
alley because the boys outside would play ball during Mass; he also
delivers sermons larded with all the eschatological terrors and permits no courting or company keeping in his parish. In all this Madden has succeeded in driving all the young people from the area,
which is plainly more depopulated than the parish of Father
O'Hara, a priest he obviously dislikes. But the local people have
their own explanation for the decay of the parish which is quite
different from the narrator's quick observation, "religion is hunting
life to the death." As a young man Madden had found couples
keeping company in the parish, a practice he deplored because of
his conviction that the idealism of the Irish people belongs in religion, not in sex; and in particular he found fault with the high-
spirited Julia Cahill. When Julia cared not at all for his repeated
injunctions and even laughed in his face, Madden in an excess of
choler delivered a foaming denunciation from the pulpit which led
to Julia's expulsion from her own house and a subsequent existence

with a blind, old woman on the edge of the bog. Julia left for America under somewhat mysterious circumstances, but on the day of her departure it is reported that she cursed the village which has seen a steady decline of population ever since.

The narrator is sympathetic but naturally skeptical. His gentle question about the efficacy of any curse provokes an energetic rejoinder:

Didn't she go every night into the mountains? She was seen one night over yonder, and the mountains are ten miles off, and whom would she have gone to see except the fairies? And who could have given her the power to curse the village?

This refusal to sort out two kinds of explanation for the events of popular narrative resembles the attitude taken by W. B. Yeats in his collection of stories, *The Celtic Twilight;* Moore read these stories with delight and reviewed them appreciatively, as he did Yeats's later collection *The Secret Rose.* Significantly one of the things Father Madden is opposed to is all talk about "pagan Ireland" and folklore, subjects for which Yeats was well known at the time. Moore evidently had Yeats well in mind when he was working on this story, for he had his publisher send proofs of the original version to the poet for correction with the note that Yeats would do the corrections much better than he. Yeats's belief in a vital, pagan Ireland, which lives in the midst of Christianity and waits for its own rebirth as Christianity inevitably fades, is conjecturally the source of Moore's published optimism for the Celtic Revival, although Moore was inclined to see an esthetic program rather than a pattern of belief as the goal of that revival. Certainly John Rodney's comment in the very first story, "the moment art, especially sculpture, passes out of the domain of the folk tale it becomes pagan," is entirely consonant with what Moore must have heard many times from Yeats. Nineteen hundred and two, the year when many of these stories were written, was also the last year of Moore's friendship with Yeats: henceforth, Moore's attitude to the Irish Renaissance was progressively more hostile, in step with his attitude to Yeats, and the revisions to the stories are marked from this point with a pronounced negativism to Irish life.

Irish memories are long, and recalling Moore's profoundly unpatriotic *Parnell and His Ireland,* critics in Dublin had little to say

about the 1902 Gaelic translation of *The Untilled Field*. But when
the full English version appeared in 1903, reviewers in London,
while a little quizzical about a work obviously not destined for Saxon
readers, were generally very taken with the book, praising it for its
economy and precision of detail. Moore had already told his publisher that *The Untilled Field* contained some of his best work, and
he was undoubtedly right, although the boast was an old refrain for
him and sometimes used to announce his weakest efforts. Apart
from the very real distinction of some of the stories, the collection is
held together as a unit by thematic development and repetition: the
notion of exile appears again and again, as does the life-hating nature
of Catholicism, the subconscious materialism of the priests, and the
need to find intense artistic and personal experience in the ordinary
and habitual scenes of daily life. Reference has been made already to
the influence of Yeats in one story and to the widely claimed
influence of Turgenev on the whole book; but *The Untilled Field* is,
as a collection, much denser and more unified than the work of
either of these writers. In its ability to generate a complex vision of a
culture from a finite number of situations repeated and varied, it is a
new genre, one looking not backwards, but forwards to the similar
methods of Joyce's *Dubliners*. Joyce's book is indebted to Moore as a
series of sketches depicting Irishmen limited by Church and culture
from total self-realization as men or artists. *Dubliners* is mostly
urban in setting, whereas *The Untilled Field* is generally rural, although in both the figure of the priest or the lay celibate dominated
by rather than dominating his environment is prominent.

IV The Lake

Originally planned as a companion story to those in *The Untilled
Field, The Lake* grew in length until it developed as a separate
novel. Still, in many ways it resembles those other stories, sharing
with "Julia Cahill's Curse" the tale of a priest denouncing a girl from
the pulpit, with "Home Sickness" the mysterious and inexorable call
to exile, with "A Letter to Rome" the celibate's uncomprehending
fascination with sensuality, with "So On He Fares" the tendency to
regard the later events of a life as transformations of earlier experiences, with "The Exile" the fugitive complexity of human, as opposed to spiritual, relationships. And yet it is a book with a peculiar
life of its own, quite apart from the consideration that here, unlike
the first edition of *The Untilled Field*, the intent is to encourage the

active man's determination to leave Ireland as an uncongenial locale for a free and creative existence.

One can gain some idea of the peculiar atmosphere of *The Lake* from a reading of the often-esteemed first lines:

It was one of those enticing days at the beginning of May when white clouds are drawn about the earth like curtains. The lake lay like a mirror that someone had breathed upon, the brown islands showing through the mist faintly, with gray shadows falling into the water, blurred at the edges. The ducks were talking softly in the reeds, the reeds themselves were talking; and the water lapped softly about the smooth limestone shores. But there was an impulse in the gentle day, and turning from the sandy spit, Father Oliver walked to and fro along the disused cart-track about the edge of the wood, asking himself if he were going home, knowing quite well that he could not bring himself to interview his parishioners that morning.

For a man who spent a great deal of ink on defining his critical reactions to the Impressionist painters, and who often clinched arguments with the recollection that he had actually known some of the Impressionists, to create this scene will seem entirely characteristic. It is an attempt to render a complex emotional state through the perception of visual details which, however, become unreliable as soon as they are invoked—the islands which are reflected into gray shadows, blurring out of sharp focus; the mist; the clouds. Yet this pictorial detail is important not in its own right but as the visual equivalent of an attitude to the external world in which everything is bathed in a pervasive mental fluid which is no longer separable from that external world. Hence the animism—the ducks talking, the reeds talking, the lake, in a complicated image, suggesting not only reflected breath but the life which breath implies. Father Oliver is not only present in landscape, but he exists in an organic continuum with it as he responds to the "impulse" of the bright spring day.

But in proportion as he is implicated in this beautiful world, Father Gogarty becomes more estranged from that life for which he has been trained. In lingering among the trees and reeds which line Lough Carra, Gogarty is at the same time neglecting his parish for the moment and abandoning the framework of books and theoretical precepts which constitutes his public self. It is not clear where Father Gogarty is thinking of when he asks himself if he is going home, for syntactically the phrase applies indifferently to the interviewing of parishioners or the walk along the wood: the word "home" is an important one in the novel, occurring at moments of decision, as in Gogarty's subsequent choice for exile, "home is not always where we are born," or Rose Leicester's "London is my natural home" after her departure from Ireland. Gogarty's words are to be found in an extended comparison to the migratory bird which must leave or die. But already, in this initial passage, the ducks are present, floating on the water, a symbol of the flight which must inevitably take place when the priest fully understands the terms offered him by this beckoning landscape, when he perceives that it is a sort of exile to remain among those whose ideas or instincts are alien.

The Lake is dedicated to Edouard Dujardin, whose influence can be detected in numerous ways beyond the new perfection Moore brought to the interior monologue technique inherited from his French friend. Dujardin was the author of a book, *La Source du Fleuve Chrétien*, demonstrating the dynamic character of religious beliefs as they evolve in time; Moore has Rose Leicester become involved in London with Ralph Ellis, a man whose *Source of the Christian River* shares not only the title, but also the same preoccupations as Dujardin's. (This coy playing with names is carried to unusual lengths in the novel: Oliver Gogarty seems to be christened merely as a pleasantry aimed at Moore's neighbor, the famous doctor and writer; Ralph Ellis suggests perhaps Ashton Ellis, the translator of Wagner, and hence a man with considerable relevance to Dujardin and his enthusiasm for the German composer.)

But perhaps Moore is most indebted to Dujardin's comparison of time to a river, for throughout *The Lake* there is an ongoing contrast between Lough Carra, whose tideless waters suggest the static contemplation of self possessed by the hermit Marban, whom Gogarty studies so intently, and the eternally progressing waters of a river or occasionally the unconfined currents of the sea. Oliver Gogarty spends his whole life around the shores of the lake, but when he decides to depart it is by crossing over the water in an immersion he compares to baptism. In the opening chapter, still fascinated by the lake, Oliver sees a boat plying its waters and immediately he says that were he on such a boat, it would not be on a lake but on the bright sea, out of sight of land. Note, too, that in the passage already quoted, the image of the lake as a mirror reflecting breath does indeed suggest life, but in a context uniquely associated with the moment of death. Guilt, death, stasis—all these are by long association linked by Moore with the religious mind; no wonder that the lake is in legend the haunt of the reclusive holy man Marban, or that Oliver must leave the lake when he ceases to be a priest.

Not only a priest, but something of a historian with an interest in the past less scholarly yet as keen as that of Ralph Ellis, Gogarty is at work on a study of the hermit Marban and his brother Guaire the king. In the implied dialectic between the active man of affairs and the withdrawn ascetic fearful of change there are to be found two halves of a dilemma, the whole of which is life, and which effectively divides the personnel of the novel into two groups—those with the steady unchanging vision of Marban, like Oliver's sister the Mother Superior, and those whose attitude to experience is as free and flexible as that of Rose Leicester. Only Oliver Gogarty manages to make the transition from one group to the other, from stasis to kinesis. (Like very many of Moore's novels *The Lake* concerns itself primarily with the question of vocation, the role one is to seek in life, a topic which, from its frequency and prominence, one would judge to be his favorite.)

Oliver, in reviewing his life, is prone to find his first inclination to the priesthood in his aversion to the thought of living his life in the company of Annie McGrath, his childhood friend. In Ireland such a dislike of marriage may be taken as the strongest kind of evidence for a religious vocation, but it is clear that Oliver, while a bachelor with all the bachelor's mistrust of personal relationships, is not one who finds women repugnant. Rather, it is the diurnal monotony of living each day in the family shop which is abhorrent, for Oliver is heavily inclined toward adventure and uncommon experience, spending his time as a child reading of robbers and pirates. When his sister Eliza enters the convent, Oliver suddenly changes his reading to the lives of saints, and from this moment he develops a fully conscious resolve for religious life because he sees a new kind of adventure in "saints who by renouncement of animal life had contrived to steal up to the last bounds, where they could see the eternal life that lies beyond the grave." By a simple transformation the attractions offered by the pirates as a release from conventional life have become the adventures of saints and priests who offer no less striking an alternative, and one more realistic; curiously the phrasing of the earlier reading has been carried over to the later, with its saints who steal up to the last bounds of experience like pirates to some fortress. At Maynooth Oliver's quest for the unusual and romantic manifests itself when, to the consternation of the seminary professors and the hostile amusement of his fellow students, he tries to achieve the extreme asceticism of the saints by a course of rigid diets and scourging. This is discouraged. But when Oliver Gogarty is ordained, he uses his influence with the bishop to obtain a position as pastor of the poorest parish in Connaught, a post of great solitude and poverty he retains until he is transferred to Garranard some time before the events in the narrative take place.

Whether by inexperience, by submerged attraction to Rose Leicester, who certainly entrances him, or by simple clerical insensitivity, Oliver reacts with great severity when he finds that Rose, the parish schoolteacher, is pregnant, condemning Rose from the pulpit and driving her from the parish with such vehemence that his remorse occupies a good part of the initial narrative. It is certain that, as with Father Madden of "Julia Cahill's Curse" or even Mrs. Barfield from *Esther Waters,* religion acts as an alienating force with Gogarty, causing him to lose any inclination to pity or humane feelings in an outpouring of moral preachments (in this connection a significant detail is the dream Oliver has of Rose drowning in the lake which reunites the lake with its multiple associations of religion, death, and guilt). Later Gogarty's official, clerical self causes him to respond harshly to the human needs of his sister Mary, who complains of the hardships of convent life; and the dereliction is the more remarkable in that Gogarty's career somewhat resembles that of the volatile Mary with her various vocations of shop-assistant, nursery governess, musical student, rabbit farmer, and nun.

Father Oliver is relieved as well as chastened upon receipt of a letter from a London priest who reproves him for his excessive behavior but supplies the information that Rose is well. Most of the remainder of the novel consists of an interspersion of Oliver's reflections as a sort of accompaniment to the prolonged exchange of letters between the priest and Rose Leicester. Moore had several times found things to praise in the work of Samuel Richardson, father of the epistolary novel, often comparing the psychological interests he shared with Turgenev and Dujardin to the achievements of the eighteenth-century novelist. But what Richardson accomplished he had perhaps done once for all time. Despite touches of dexterity in defining the opposing views and sensibilities of his two writers, Moore nowhere gives promise of enlarging the pair of Smollett and Richardson to a trinity by his own mastery of the epistolary form; and he is consequently exposed to the longueurs, the slowness of movement, and the sheer inactivity to which that form sometimes lends itself. Still he knows what he is about: judging from her letters, often written hurriedly and in the emotion of the moment, Rose is animated by feelings ranging from friendly condescension to amused contempt; Oliver on the other hand is more deliberate, more earnest. Yet of the two it is evidently Rose who possesses the greater awareness of herself from the beginning. Oliver gains consciousness of his own motives by going through the process of writing these letters, which thus form the counterpart of the moments of introspection and insight that mark Gogarty's movement to possession of self.

In the disentangling of motives that follows the exchange of letters, Father Oliver at first thinks that he is attracted to Rose because he loves her, not realizing that he is seeking not a person, but a symbol, an idea (although perhaps since friends always occupy this role for Moore, especially in *Hail and Farewell* and *Confessions of a Young Man*, the distinction need not be elaborated). Rose, as her name suggests, is associated with flowers, the enjoyment of experience beyond the narrow limits set by conventional life. Hence Oliver thinks of Rose as a flower living among grimy London tenements; on another occasion he hopes that living near the convent in Tinnick will somehow produce a longing for color in the local people that will lead to the planting of flowers; and again his thoughts are driven to Rose Leicester when he reflects that flowers are the only beautiful things available to poor people, especially roses which are "within reach of all." Rose herself thinks that Gogarty's already confined life is limited still further by his reading of *The Imitation of Christ*, by Thomas A Kempis, which reminds her of "a flower growing in the shadow of a cloister, dying for lack of sun"; for her, too, the rose represents the freshness of further experience. Finally Oliver realizes that he is drawn not to Rose but to an abstraction, an idea; and that this idea, which demands the separation from his past life and from his own country, is nothing other than the quest for life. Rose is a necessary symbol for Gogarty, but to become satisfied with a familiar relationship with Rose Leicester would be as fatal as that old, habitual uniformity once promised by a life with Annie McGrath in the grocery business. When Oliver leaves Garranard to confront his fate, he is alone, as lonely as any hermit; yet he is no longer content to remain by the lake, the hermit's locale. He crosses over, not denying anything that has gone before, but transforming it, facing the future with the resources he has drawn from the past.

Reviewers of the time found evidence that *The Lake* showed that Moore was moving even further from Naturalism (which was praised), that there was more in Father Gogarty's correspondence than one expected from a priest writing to an unmarried lady (which was condemned), and that the novel was written in an unfamiliar style (which was misunderstood). In general, criticism was divided between appreciation of the lyrical treatment of Irish landscape and perplexity at the artificiality and prolixity involved in the adoption of the epistolary form, criticism which, however, was in the main so favorable that Moore overcame his earlier misgivings and wrote to his friends that he had had a success. James Joyce, who read this novel and knew both Moore and the original Oliver Gogarty, was derisive about the conclusion of the novel, which describes Gogarty's buttocks shining in the moonlight as he prepares to swim the lake. Later Joyce parodied this scene several times in the St. Kevin episodes of *Finnegans Wake,* although he limited his criticisms at the time to scornful comments made in letters to his brother. And yet Joyce was in a sense more right than the reviewers, for Gogarty often *is* a comical figure: Moore's characters seem to learn by progressing through stages in which they pursue an idea to an absurd extreme before making the necessary transition to the next stage. This is the key to the unsteady advance of the hero-narrators of *Confessions of a Young Man* and, pre-eminently, of *Hail and Farewell.*

V Hail and Farewell

Oliver Gogarty's comment in *The Lake* that little is ever finished in Ireland, that innumerable bright beginnings are crowned with just as many failures, could be taken not only as a summary of Moore's stay in Dublin, but as the central theme of *Hail and Farewell.* As he prepares to leave England, Moore recalls two other occasions when he had thought to make literature from a residence in Ireland: the time when as a "magnificent young Montmartrian" he had thought of renting a house in the Dublin mountains to compose a romantic story; and a time, later by ten years, when inspired by talk of a new revival in Ireland, he had dreamed of working on a novel to be titled "Ruin and Weed." Neither work is completed, the failure in each case attributable to the land of ruins and dereliction which inspired them. *Hail and Farewell* is, in a sense, a reprise of these earlier undertakings (thus furnishing one of the many interpretations of the title); with them it shares the primacy of art as a motivation for residence, a vision of Ireland as inimical to creative existence, and the cycle of enthusiastic hopes followed by radical disillusionment.

Moore tinkered with his title several times in the process of composition, indicating early that this was to be his farewell to Ireland, but later developing a more complex viewpoint which united Catullus' *ave* and *vale* and the history of his own dealings with his native country as a diagnosis of the promise, yet the enforced barrenness of Ireland. In the first place "hail" and "farewell" are seen as correlative: he hails Ireland when he is saying good-bye to England; and as he leaves Ireland he rejoices to be returning to the land of Anglo-Saxon Protestantism. For Moore, the opinions reached in *Hail and Farewell* mark a return of another sort, to the conclusions arrived at in *Parnell and His Island* some thirty years before, conclusions which unite the country's sterility of culture with the irreparable disappearance of the feudal order (and from this may be constructed a rule by which to test people like Yeats, who wish to return to a fixed past which has vanished forever: "hail" coupled with "farewell" is an assertion of change). Nothing is static, all is fluid. The lesson that Moore had taught in *The Lake* and *Confessions of a Young Man* is also operative here where it helps explain his dealings with other people, who are cultivated in proportion as they are useful for the moment, dropped when that usefulness seems to have passed, and taken up again when a new function has been divined for them.

Moore had been speaking in the main of his own experiences in *Confessions of a Young Man*, yet he had, for purposes of publication, changed his name to Edwin Dayne, and that of Lewis Weldon Hawkins to Lewis Ponsonby Marshall, retaining real names only for very minor or celebrated figures. But in *Hail and Farewell* he disguises neither himself nor any of his acquaintances; he drags the luminaries of literary Dublin into unwilling collaboration with him, finding in their interrelationships the patterns of art. Still the focus is very much upon Moore himself, whom he defines by pursuing his elusive self through these experiences. (Moore does not idly make the comparison to the work of Rousseau in *Ave*, the first volume of *Hail and Farewell*; for like Rousseau he is interested less in describing the tables and chairs of existence than in weaving "a net woven of fine silk for the capture of dreams, memories, hopes, aspirations, sorrows, with here and there a secret shame.") As early as the first poems he had regarded narrative as doubly creative, for it generates not only a story but also the man who tells the story, who is created by a correlative process, is mirrored by the story he tells. Discovery of self and creation of self are, by this account, not so very different. If the Moore presented in *Hail and Farewell* is sometimes too conveniently naive, or on other occasions rather better provided with apt sayings than one would expect, it is because like the rest of his fiction he has been harmonized with the text, become part of the only pattern that will make these events comprehensible; for memory is a process of reconstruction which, by definition, imposes a conceptual framework not available at the time of the actual experiences. Memory, like art, is a sort of process of detachment by which one truly recognizes past occurrences in the act of discarding them; to bid them farewell is to greet them for the first time in their objective form.

Why would a man who had written so vituperatively of Ireland in *Parnell and His Island* and returned so energetically to the task in this book, should ever have wanted to go to Ireland at all in 1901? A variety of reasons are offered: revulsion over British participation in the Boer War, the ugliness of England, a personal change of values in which he hates his former self as much as he now hates England (a useful insight, since in *Confessions of a Young Man* such violent reversals usually betoken a change in artistic allegiance). With a hint of the polemics to be brandished later, Moore also recalls that at this point art and literature had ceased to interest him, by which the alert reader is to understand that a very propitious moment to revisit Ireland has arrived. But the most significant detail involves not a conscious reason but a method of argument. Speaking of his growing abhorrence of things English, the novelist formulates this contention: "the detestable race has produced nothing original; not one sculptor, nor a great painter, except, perhaps, John Millais. He came from one of the Channel Islands. A Frenchman!" The absurdities of the statement are too manifest to warrant comment; but it is important to recognize that formally it is the exact counterpoint of the later argument by which Moore denies that Ireland, under the influence of Catholicism, has itself ever produced anything original. The two claims not only balance, but also to some extent neutralize, each other. Each is written in a kind of excess of conviction, an argument carried to an extreme, and thus an absurd, limit; although it is hard not to feel that the irrationality of the first position is much greater than that of the second.

To explain the agitation that drove him to Ireland, Moore relates that one day in a walk through Chelsea, meditating on the Boer War, he entered Hospital Road and suddenly heard a voice commanding him to go to Ireland. Of this burlesque commission possibly the most significant detail is Moore's insistence that no one was near him at the time: Britain's most famous agnostic *may* have received a divine injunction, but it is far more likely that the source of the inspiration was a delusion, a psychological quirk, a momentary enchantment. This enchantment or delusion Moore experiences on other occasions, and uses to account for his collaboration with Yeats on the play *Diarmuid and Grania,* written, so he says, on the plan of a translation of the original text by Moore into French, a translation of the French text into English by Lady Gregory, a translation of the English text into Irish by a native speaker, a translation of the Irish back into English by Lady Gregory, and some stylistic polish finally added by Yeats. The ancient Irish thought of love as a sort of spell, distracting a man from his normal equilibrium, and in the play Grania exercises this sort of influence to convert the heroic Diarmuid to a conventional farmer: Moore often speaks of his return to Ireland as the result of Grania's spell, which is thus, as in the source, a mythical way of externalizing a puzzling, internal impulse. Another motif which is nothing more than the working out of this same kind of personal quirk is to be found in the many references to another enchantress from Irish mythology, Niamh, whose call to Usheen to "come away" bears some resemblance to the mysterious call Moore heard in Hospital Road (in particular this motif is used in reference to George Russell, summoned as a young man to the service of occult philosophy, and to Lady Gregory, whose siren calls for W. B. Yeats are archly satirized by Moore).

But the voice commanding George Moore to Ireland is most properly associated with the conversion of St. Paul, who also heard a voice which helped him overcome his habitual prejudice against his own people. While working on *Hail and Farewell,* the novelist wrote a play, *The Apostle,* in which Paul's conversion is seen to be a delusion, since Christ has neither died nor risen again; Paul's preaching of the arrival of the Messiah is mistaken, just as Moore is mistaken about the rebirth of Ireland; likewise Paul in the midst of his enthusiasm is quixotic, as quixotic as Moore in his hopes for quarrying literature from a priest-ridden country. In Moore's play Jesus and Paul meet many years after the supposed events of the Resurrection; but Christ's story only infuriates Paul, who kills him as a heretic. Thus Paul's career has come full cycle, to the days when he killed Christians as heretics before his conversion. Paul's return to the patterns of his youth is very like the spiralling trajectory of Moore's attitudes to Ireland in *Hail and Farewell*, but in a complicating development he also resembles Christ. *The Apostle* makes Christ and Paul complementary figures, different possibilities of the same personality, since Christ, too, once dreamed of a vision of his election by God, and had a career of a "magnificent young heretic" opposed to the Jewish establishment before his retirement to the monastery: Paul in middle age is like Christ in youth. This interest in the reciprocal relationship of individuals is relevant to the technique of *Hail and Farewell*, as will be seen; and it explains what otherwise would be difficult to explain—why Moore hears the voice of Paul's commission, but interprets it to mean that it is he who is the Messiah born to lead Ireland from slavery to the priests and moralizers.

This intrusion of the Messianic hope for Moore comes only after he has seen a number of redeemers proposed for Ireland, all equally delusory and ineffective. At a dinner at the Shelbourne Hotel he sees a gallery of such discredited saviors, beginning with T. W. Rolleston, described as a "Messiah that punctured while the others were going by on inflated tyres"; George Russell, rejected by Moore as a Messiah because he is not interested in the Irish language; Edward Martyn, who "believes himself to be the Messiah—he who will give Ireland literature and her political freedom." But in discussing with T. P. Gill the political future of Ireland, Moore begins to formulate for himself a notion of the true savior as he who will save Ireland from Catholicism, a being quite different from the accepted notion of the popular leader surrendering Ireland to "an eternal singing of 'The Wearin' o' the Green.' " Convinced that the Messiah will need to de-Catholicize Ireland and finding himself called to that task, Moore decides to write an autobiography, a "sacred book" which will awaken Ireland from the sleep of centuries. (The ambition is best understood in connection with Moore's contention in the preface to *The Apostle* that The Acts of the Apostles is Paul's own autobiography, drawing its power from Paul's account of himself as a man.) As a confirmation of this mission the novelist one day hears another voice (but this time indisputably from within) urging him to put aside any thought of buying a house "because *Hail and Farewell* must be written." With the thought of this book of liberation, Moore's sojourn in Ireland and the account which contains it are brought to a conclusion; and his long-delayed hopes of writing a novel about the ruins and weeds of Irish life are triumphantly fulfilled.

If Moore's errand is ultimately a circular one, to visit Ireland in order to redeem it by seeking a conspicuous exile to be advertised as loudly as possible in a triple-decker autobiography, it follows that a great deal of the significance of what he sees is originally opaque to him, for his mission only becomes clear after his initial optimism has passed. Hence solely with the ironic perspective of hindsight can he appreciate Edward Martyn's opinion that Gaelic and Catholicism go hand in hand, a notion that causes the recorder Moore, though not the participant Moore, to realize that Gaelic is as necessarily dispensable as the religion of those who speak it. Again, as he approaches Dublin by the night steamer, Moore is put in mind of the legend that the ancient inhabitants of Ireland were able to make the country seem as small as a pig's back to her enemies or as a land of great enchantment to her enemies; but to his consternation he sees both omens at once. This duality of vision is perfectly explicable in terms of the precise nature of his redemptive task, a task he is soon to appreciate when he complains to Yeats that "at present Ireland isn't bigger than a priest's back."

But, as in *The Untilled Field*, Ireland is regarded less as a place than as a condition of spirit to be found in its inhabitants. Moore finds evidence of this in his brother Maurice, who seems unable to take any idea to its conclusion, whether it is the education of his sons in the Irish language, his defense of Catholicism (in which he is tricked into admitting that Cardinal Newman's account of the conversion in *Apologia Pro Vita Sua* contains some very poor writing), or his Irish patriotism (sustained by a career in the British army). Moore's contention is that Irish Catholicism, soft and peaty as the climate, muddies the minds of those who profess it, leading them to absurdities and contradictions. Here the prime example is Edward Martyn, the source of John Norton in *Mike Fletcher*, already pointed out by Harding in that novel as a contradictory character.

Martyn seems to have a genuine creative gift, patriotism, an urge to founded a lasting Irish literature, and yet he allows himself to be deflected by religious considerations, proposing to resign his directorship in the Irish Literary Theatre when *The Countess Cathleen* is condemned by a cardinal who has not troubled himself to see it. Again, though his play *The Heather Field* is fine and original work, he falls into difficulties with *The Tale of a Town*, in which he lacks the coherence to hold the drama together, provoking Moore's wondering comment that even a baby can handle a plot, if there be one. Edward, with his heavy, round face is often visualized as a baby with a baby's simple range of behavior. His alarm at the moral effect of *The Countess Cathleen* is anesthetized by T. P. Gill, who quietens him by the assurance that other priests might have other opinions: "I more or less understood that Gill's voice is low and musical, that he had sung 'Hush-a-bye baby on the tree top'; but a public scandal might awaken the baby again." With his total allegiance to religion (which Moore dismisses as a reliance on magic), Martyn has only a child's perception of things outside that world; and he falls again and again into naive recitation of formulas, as, for example, when he explains his enthusiasm for the cathedral at Aix by saying that Gothic windows are pointed whereas the Romanesque are round.

Yet, after all, Maurice Moore and Edward Martyn were old acquaintances, Irish types to be sure, but known to the novelist long before the time of his hopes for Irish literature. In the discussion of *The Untilled Field* it was suggested that Moore's optimism for the Irish Renaissance almost exactly coincides with the period of his esteem for W. B. Yeats, and it does seem that, as the most considerable figure in this movement, Yeats is the one most unremittingly subjected to hostile analysis. Even before his removal to Dublin Moore suspects that Yeats, whom he has admired as the author of *The Celtic Twilight* and *The Sacred Rose*, is tapering off in his recent work into the vague indications of Mallarmé; hence his remark that "all the Irish movement rose out of Yeats and returns to Yeats" is subtly ambiguous, since it implies that both are prone to the same thinness, the same bloodless idealism. But art is never bloodless; it depends upon the heart as much as upon the head, or so Moore claims in his Dublin lecture to introduce the Hugh Lane exhibition of Impressionist paintings, a lecture vital to the understanding of *Hail and Farewell* because it contains the standards by which artists are to be judged. Manet's art was "all Manet," neither mere pictorial theorizing nor a series of borrowings from other painters. Yeats, on the other hand, is too much the metaphysician, the man of ideas, and his art suffers, while his inability to put himself rather than some mere artistic pose into his work makes him nothing more than a literary fop. (Moore is being consistent here, but he is also acidly repaying an unpleasant memory, since Yeats had called *Moore's* mind too argumentative and abstract.)

As Moore repeatedly emphasizes, there are many analogies to be drawn between the black-gowned dialectician Yeats, a sort of monk of poetry, and the sober and pietistic Edward Martyn. Both share a belief in ritual, whether Catholicism or Rosicrucianism; both are seen to be decreasing, not increasing, in creative vitality; both are narrow and limited in their human sympathies. The great lesson that Moore claims to find in Manet is that "art is praise of life," but neither Yeats nor Martyn is able to acquiesce in the simple beauty of the birds swimming at Stephen's Green which so much entrances the novelist. Yeats is an idealist, but the word premises a limitation as well as a hint of admiration: the sensation Moore has of floating in the air while Yeats is speaking does not compensate for the heartless detachment implicit in such a separation from the transactions of ordinary life. It need scarcely be elaborated that for Moore, who has written of the importance of the sensibility of the artist in a long series of studies from *A Modern Lover* to "Mildred Lawson," such a limitation is a disqualifying impediment for an artist.

There is a great deal of comedy to be found in the comparison between Yeats's ascetic espousal of the notion that the artist must make sacrifices, be unworldly, and the poet's frequent disappearances into bun shops with female admirers, or the pampering he receives at Coole from Lady Gregory, but it is *comédie larmoyante*. Like *Hail and Farewell* itself, it is comedy that arises from a certain kind of failure, the failure of good intentions to realize themselves in a genuine art movement, the failure of artists to be sufficiently serious about art to succeed, and most of all, the inevitable failure of Ireland to rise above its bovine acceptance of disabilities of spirit which make such farcical adventures a foregone conclusion.

Most readers of *Hail and Farewell* have been interested in the malicious reportage rather than the form of the novel, although Moore himself said that his book was much different than a mere work of gossip. At the time of the appearance of the first edition, it was fashionable to link Moore's name with that of Laurence Sterne, with whom genuine affinities can be detected; but these are only affinities, and Moore's only too credible claim that he had not read Sterne should suffice to lay that kind of criticism to rest. Whatever the overt model (and Moore's whole career shows that his reliance on specific influences is always to be taken with a grain of salt), *Hail and Farewell* remains one of Moore's freshest and most enduring performances, a masterpiece of the narrative form. It may well seem that Moore was wrong about the future of the Irish Renaissance, but about its character he was not mistaken; he saw only too well that the aristocratic idealism of Yeats and the ecclesiastical idealism of Martyn left out too much of common experience to give rise to a genuine, native tradition. The earthiness, cynicism, and sly humor of subsequent Irish writers from Joyce to Frank O'Connor owe much more to the kind of vision to be found in the work of George Moore than to the conscious gentility of Coole Park.

CHAPTER 5

Last Novels

I The Brook Kerith

THE great lesson that Moore claimed to have learned from
Wagner is that Wagner's style is "all melody"; that is, the
technique of the operas operates so as to join the elements of narration and musical setting on the level of the individual notes, the
simplest units of composition. Moore first came across this
technique in the work of the French novelist Edouard Dujardin,
who was trying to make use of Wagner's form but who was unaware
of the style's psychological possibilities. Able to see that the flowing
uninterrupted narrative made possible by this technique was ideally
suited for description of the flow of thoughts and impressions within
the human mind, Moore was thus one of the inventors of the
"stream of consciousness" technique later used by such writers as
James Joyce and Virginia Woolf.

Moore's own use of the literary motif and the stream-of-consciousness technique can both be traced back to Wagner, as can his
discussion of "the melodic line" in *Conversations in Ebury Street*, a
discussion in which it is argued that anecdotes and digressions in a
narrative should be molded in order to cast light on the central
thread of the story. But in his later work the musical analogy is
enlarged to include the sonorities of texture. Speaking again of
Wagner, Moore observes that in his letters the musician produces
sentences with such a control of sound that seemingly they roll on
forever. Not all of Moore's readers have admired his adoption of this
facet of Wagner's genius (even though it should be pointed out that
Moore was already moving in this direction in his published admiration for the work of Walter Pater, or in his opinion that conscious
style was necessary to put back into a language what had been taken
out by custom and repetition); some critics, indeed, have been

138

genuinely inclined to condemn this style as a pernicious superfluity. George Bernard Shaw was heard to say that such was the self-sustaining impetus of the method that there was no reason why Moore could not continue *The Brook Kerith* for another fifty thousand or even fifty million pages. Yet in its capacity for capturing the endless flexibility of the human mind as it reflects upon the similarities of diverse experiences compounded and recast into new forms in every stage of life, the style is able, no doubt, to do what Moore hoped for it. Of its nature the technique is more finely attuned to mental, than to physical, events, a fact that inevitably loses for it the allegiance of a substantial portion of its potential audience; yet it unquestionably marks the moment at which George Moore attains a voice which is uniquely and evidently his own.

From *Hail and Farewell* it is clear that the need to find a prophet will sooner or later lead to the displacement of that longing to oneself. Hence Joseph of Arimathea in *The Brook Kerith* not only becomes a disciple of Jesus, but after Jesus' "death," he in a sense replaces him, going up to Jerusalem to be slain by the Zealots; in the same way Paul preaches his version of Christ's story and moves on to Rome and his own death. But it is more than the psychology of the Messiah that is owed to the time of the Dublin period, for in the preface to *The Apostle* it is related that from John Eglinton came the account of a recent French book in which it was argued that Christ suffered not death, but merely a cataleptic swoon on the cross. *The Brook Kerith* offers a historical explanation which explains the religious deformation of Ireland's national character as depicted in Moore's Irish books, in which an explicit but arbitrary code of inherited morality is made to crush all inclinations to art and beauty. (Father Gogarty of *The Lake* would have done well to have listened to the theorizings of his assistant Father Moran, who was of the opinion that in their obsession with moral ideas, the Irish most resemble the ancient Jews.) There is, finally, another legacy of the Irish conversion and subsequent repentance of George Moore which is to be found in the pronounced oral character of the "melodic line"; Moore customarily dictated his later works in order to preserve the fluidity of the spoken word he had come to respect in his contact with Irish storytellers, and at least part of the effect of his later prose is traceable to those earlier influences.

Joseph of Arimathea as a boy hears the story of the election of Saul by the vision of the prophet Samuel and immediately expresses the wish to become a prophet, a wish somewhat hard of achievement in view of his youth and ignorance of Hebrew. But he will not be dissuaded (even by Samuel's poor luck in the choice of a hero which somewhat parallels his own later choice of Jesus) and survives four unsuccessful tutors in the Hebrew language until he finds an instructor named Azariah. Azariah arrives apparently by chance, just as Saul had arrived apparently by chance, for what is common to these mystic selections is the determination of the seeker rather than any outstanding qualities of the one found; but he does transfer to the boy a knowledge of the language as well a theology that causes the boy to feel regret for his natural joy at the beauty of the world and of life. Joseph's father, Dan, had been afraid that exposure to the teachings of Azariah would estrange Joseph from his own family, and it does seem that the espousal of religious enthusiasm in *The Brook Kerith* entails a corresponding distaste for the realities of sexuality and family life. Something capricious in Joseph's nature causes him to need "a hero, true or false," but makes it difficult for him to sustain any one commitment. He lives for a while with the ascetic Essenes, who attract him by their renunciation of ordinary life, and it is while living in this community that he is told that he has the full, Jewish mind, "interested in moral ideas rather than beauty"; and the conjecture cannot be far wrong, for, arriving at the monastery, Joseph finds that one of his reasons for choosing this life is his aversion to women.

Joseph is told of John the Baptist, another man seeking a prophet, who is working in preparation for his Messiah, Jesus of Nazareth. Although at first he does not meet Jesus, Joseph is deeply impressed by the new prophet's reported teachings, and is all the more surprised to find, at their first encounter, a rather naive village lad whose knowledge of the world is far inferior to his own. But Jesus possesses a consciousness of mission, which he derives from the Book of Daniel, just as Joseph lives under the influence of the first Book of Samuel: Jesus believes he cannot be harmed by his enemies as he brings the people back to God, a mission best accomplished by forsaking sexuality and the claims of family. (Jesus, Paul, and Joseph are all celibates. Moore in *Hail and Farewell* spoke of "the eternal masculine," the society of men without women, as tending to the production of ideas but ultimately rootless and inhuman.) Jesus' conviction that he will emerge, like Daniel, unscathed from every act of malice, is soon put to the test at Calvary where he is crucified but does not die. It is conventional for Christian theologians to read the events of the Old Testament as typological models for those of the New Testament, and thus, even from this point of view, there is something quite logical in Moore's recapitulative technique. But although Jesus does not die, he is sufficiently injured to rethink his vocation.

At the end of *Hail and Farewell* the embittered Moore had explained his enthusiasm for the Irish Renaissance by saying that all conversions are either financial, sexual, or hysterical in nature, and concluded that his own was a hysterical one, brought on by the Boer War. Like Moore, Jesus, after his enforced reassessment, returns to the opinions held before his conversion; the hysteria engendered by the Book of Daniel gives way to the passive acceptance of life which Jesus had experienced as a boy. No longer interested in changing men or destroying the present order, Jesus sees a sin in the urge to change things: the haggard Jesus before the crucifixion had urged his disciples to leave father, mother, or wife for his sake; but now he counsels devotion to one's parents in the belief that love implies acceptance of one's fellow man. Retired among the Essenes, he is thus at the point attained by Joseph of Arimathea before the conversion to Christianity; his crucifixion is a true crossover, not only for himself, but for Joseph, who dies at the hands of the Zealots in an end once anticipated for Jesus himself.

Many years later the Apostle Paul arrives at the monastery, bringing with him his central belief in the resurrection of Jesus Christ which he has been preaching throughout the world. As did Joseph and the early Jesus, he complains of a "thorn in the flesh," the allure of sexuality which he considers incompatible with a devotion to religious duties. In a characteristic phrase he calls himself "an angry soul . . . since God first separated me from my mother's womb," and thus makes manifest his conviction that God and separateness from normal, human experience are almost synonymous concepts. He is given to action, not to meditation; and he listens with wonder to the counsels of Jesus, who seems to him to resemble in his beliefs the Indian priests who teach that the urge to action is not only futile but blasphemous. Yet a man whose theology begins with the fact of death is not likely to be greatly moved by a shepherd mildly advocating the uncritical acceptance of life. Paul is the recurrent youth from Jesus' past, but the inevitable is not postponed by lucidity, and Paul leaves the monastery by the Brook Kerith for Rome and his own death.

To the surprise of almost everyone involved, *The Brook Kerith* was an immediate financial success, running into several editions; and it is one of the few of the author's books in print at the present time. Biblical criticism of the type popularized by Ernest Renan and David Strauss was still fashionable enough to provoke energetic denunciations or sympathetic appreciation of the portrait of Jesus, although at least one critic preferred the depiction of Joseph of Arimathea, shrewdly linking it to the treatment of Marius the Epicurean by Walter Pater. A number of reviewers took exception to the style of the novel, George Bernard Shaw among them; but others were inclined to praise this very feature, treating Moore for the first time as a man-of-letters on the order of the great Victorian writer-critics. Almost none perceived the qualities that give the novel true distinction, especially the subordination of all the incidents to a very few ideas, such as that of resurrection, which controls the recurrent life and death cycle of all the accounts. It is possible that *The Brook Kerith* is the most formally perfect of all of Moore's works, even though one hesitates to award it absolute supremacy because of a lack of vigor, arising possibly from the simplicity of the materials or even from its creator's advancing age, a consideration of some importance for all his later work (in 1916 George Moore was sixty-four years old).

II   A Story-Teller's Holiday

A Story-Teller's Holiday appeared in 1918, seven years after Moore's loud exit from Dublin, but in some ways it is as Irish as *Hail and Farewell*, in subject matter at least, and with *Hail and Farewell* it shares the device of a circular voyage: chapter one begins with the Irish mail train from Euston Station; chapter sixty-one rounds off the account with a return to Chelsea. Moore fortified the impression of the Celtic influence on his stories (most of which, indeed, are re-tellings of traditional tales) by issuing them in limited edition under the imprint of a Gaelic organization entirely of his own invention. This pleasant fiction is not at all at odds with Moore's aim of penetrating the process by which folk-tales arise from the primary concerns of ordinary life, by which the lying myth becomes the embodiment of an important truth. A book in which memoirs encircle the fictional elements and are presented on the same level with these elements, *A Story-Teller's Holiday* is inclined, at moments, to present even truth as if it were fiction, as in the account of "Sir Hugh" of Muchloon, who is evidently Moore's own father. As autobiographer as well as novelist Moore makes abundant use of his Irish memories; hence when he praises the "fecundity" of nature as opposed to the limited intelligence of a Turgenev, he is linking his art in his books of recollections to the spontaneous productions of the traditional storyteller. (This is not, strictly speaking, a scientifically accurate view of the storyteller or his tales, but it does appear to be Moore's view.)

At numerous points in the composition of these stories Moore enlisted the collaboration of James Stephens, whose task it was to put authentic peasant style on the dialogue, an important duty since the tales owe a great deal of their charm to the flowing, oral character of the narrative. Moore in these years was inclined to play down the achievements of J. M. Synge in peasant dialogue, even going so far as to claim that a fresh, young bumpkin like Synge could only have seized hold of peasant language by the reading of *The Untilled Field*. But the letters Moore wrote to Synge in the Dublin period tell a different story, for here Moore treats Synge with respect and an appreciation of his accomplishments. In truth Moore was deeply impressed with the experiments with the spontaneous style of oral narrative, as his collaboration with native speakers in some of his books demonstrates, and he was of the opinion that "every language is a potential literature," that the quality of a well-told story is already implicit in the smallest units of composition. (This idea bears some similarity to Moore's view of Wagner's method, and provides one further link with the German composer, who was even more interested than the novelist in the genesis of traditional stories.)

On the analogy of a busman's holiday a storyteller's holiday ought to be a vacation in which the fabulist is reintroduced to his craft. That this is so becomes apparent from the beginning of this voyage because, crossing the Irish Sea, the novelist recalls his invocation of Greek mythology on his recent Mediterranean trip and betrays an interest in the origin of even these stories: "Do not all mythologies rely upon the union of divinity with a mortal; and does not Deity in all the mythologies take the form of some beast or bird?" Even the most casual reader is inclined to murmur "Yeats" on seeing this theory, and it does seem that the best way to account for Moore's espousal of this view is to recall his long conversations with Yeats on Irish mythology during the composition of their jointly-written play, *Diarmuid and Grania*. Yet there is an interest to be traced here beyond the question of the specific source of one idea because Moore is announcing an important theme to be developed in all these tales: the strongly human or even primitive quality of all encounters with the divine (it will be seen that this is not a new argument for the novelist—witness Alice Barton's inability in *A Drama in Muslin* to take seriously the Christmas tableau as "a drama so obviously of human invention"). Certainly Moore shares with Yeats the comparativist bent of his treatment of traditional tales; in the retelling of "God's Grandfather," for example, he compares the mysteriously born child to Bacchus and then to Hippolytus. It should not be forgotten, too, that Yeats was a prodigious collector of folktales, and the author, in *The Celtic Twilight*, of some remarkable folklike concoctions which take the same complex and quizzical attitude to truth, fiction, and authorship as does Moore in *A Story-Teller's Holiday*.

Before travelling to the West of Ireland, the novelist pauses for some time in Dublin, where he asks to see what remains of the Dublin Post Office after the British shelling in 1916, an edifice which the local operations of mythology have transformed into "the ruins." The transformation of mundane fact into the embroideries of popular fiction is not to be wondered at in what is, after all, a well-known battle; but perhaps there is something to be criticized in what Moore conceives as the self-mythologizing of Yeats, who has gone to live in a castle in Galway, "himself having become a myth from too long brooding on myths." The art of the storyteller consists of demythologizing as much as mythologizing, for it is necessary to restore the immediate human perspective from time to time: Alec Trusselby will later speak of the great hero Usheen as merely "the biggest of the lot"; Moore equally finds it necessary to do "verifications" of Yeats and other characters from *Hail and Farewell*. Confirmation is found of the predictions in *Hail and Farewell*, that novel of actuality, that Yeats is writing for himself a life of the same cloth as his poetry, that he is short-circuiting the process by which the storyteller weaves truth into legend.

Taking the train from Dublin to Westport, Moore sees from his window many examples of the eternal pair, the priest and the bullock-driver, which, as his subsequent stories show, he takes to be archetypal of Ireland. But when an elderly priest enters his compartment he is reminded of a story which is sharper and more immediate than any theory, for he has met the priest before and in a particularly unpleasant context. A neighbor of Moore's in Dublin during the period described in *Hail and Farewell* was a retired publican, Cunningham, a strange mixture of joviality and melancholy. The joviality is his own, the fruit of years in his profession and a cheerful nature; but the melancholy is given to him by his spiritual advisor, the priest who is later to share Moore's compartment. In his writing about priests Moore is inclined to fix upon the love of comfort and materialism of these professors of the unworldly, and this case is no different: holding the fires of hell as a final argument, the priest tries to get Cunningham to leave his substantial earnings to the Church. The poor Cunningham, who despairs and commits suicide, is viewed by Moore as a man only half free, a man whose conscience is in fee to an institution outside himself, and an extreme, though not unfairly chosen, representative of the plight of Ireland. The relinquishment of the right to private judgment, Moore thinks, is the cause of the untrustworthiness of the national character because there is no solid center of conduct to be found within any individual, only a constant tension between external authority and the demands of nature. In accordance with this view Moore will select stories that reflect the struggle between the individual conscience at grips with the universal human predicament and the harsh and intrusive force of external discipline.

Once in Westport Moore is given an opportunity to meet a native storyteller, the man who is to tell many of the tales of *A Story-Teller's Holiday* (but to add to the complexity, while his stories are traditional, he himself is completely fictional, a creature of the novelist). Alec Trusselby is moderately pious, yet his profession allies him rather to the forests, where he makes his home in summer, than to the conventional life of the modern Irishman. The ancient Irish storyteller was a favored guest of kings, but Trusselby, with his store of sensual tales of priests and nuns, is without a home, being forced to earn his keep in winter by repeating his stories in peasant homes. In the "Big House" he is valued only as a character, his stories drawing no interest at all from the modern counterparts of the old kings. Symbolic, perhaps, of the vanished nobility of his calling is the blackthorn club named by Alec "the Murrigan" after "a great queen" (apparently the Morrigu, the ancient Irish goddess of war);

in such difficult times Alec is obliged to prove his worth with the club on all those rash enough to challenge his dignity.

In the first of his stories Alec recounts the tale of Liadin and Curithir for his new audience, a tale that fits very nicely into the associative pattern that has been forming in Moore's mind during his journey. Thinking first of the plight of Cunningham, trapped by his religious convictions, Moore is moved to free a bee unable to find its way out of the railway carriage; then he recalls another railway journey in which he had been unable to free a nun who seemed to be appealing to him for help. Alec's story about lovers trapped by a vow imposed by a severe priest fits not only into this psychological matrix, but into the larger vision of an Ireland living in a sort of clerical prison. This technique, of adapting the telling of the story to the situation, is a characteristic of oral narrative: Moore's deployment of framing materials into larger matters of structure is the counterpart of Alec's ability to relate his story to "the druid stone" under which he is eating his lunch.

Two great poets, Liadin and Curithir, are drawn together partly for amorous, partly for professional reasons (for as poets they are complementary, his larger range of poetry balanced by the sweeter tone of her songs). At their first meeting, however, Curithir is so overcome that he is unable to remember his poetry, a strange development of the complicated relationship in Moore's work between art and sexuality. But afterwards, as the two poets resume their own journeys, it is quite different; Liadin becomes famous throughout Ireland because of the quantity of love poetry excited by her passion for Curithir. Before long the priests are outraged by the poetry and the amorous behavior that the poetry encourages. Castigating her for the "filthy, bad, black passion" which is her perennial subject, they urge her to think of old age and death, thus manifesting that familiar dichotomy for Moore: art is "praise of life"; religion is ultimately derivable to a death wish. Nevertheless, under such pressure Liadin cannot very well resist, and she is forced to take a vow to break with Curithir, a vow which results in the cessation of all her poetry. Understandably chagrinned at this arrangement, Curithir, whose own poetry inevitably declines, takes Liadin to meet Cummin, a hermit, in order to see if the vow may not be put aside. Cummin is more humane than the priests, but his counsel amounts to the same thing, that life is short and death imminent, and that they would do well to reconcile themselves to the vow, for eternal things are of more value than passing love. Yet Cummin has a novel insight in his theory that since merit is proportional to the temptation overcome, the two poets have a unique opportunity to win an eternal reward if they will lie together by night without committing sin. The lovers accede to this suggestion, perhaps because it is the only alternative to complete separation, and inevitably they are tempted, just as inevitably falling into the very sin they are supposed to avoid. Curithir is sent to Rome to obtain a pardon for the breaking of the vow; but as he leaves Liadin dies in a fall from the rock she has climbed in order to see his departure.

This story, which Moore tells through the mouth of Alec Trusselby, he had acquired from medieval Irish literature, going over it many times in discussion with the great scholar Kuno Meyer. In treatment there are nevertheless many touches that obviously are traceable to the sage of Ebury Street rather than to his predecessors from the Middle Ages. Like the very similar Héloise of *Héloise and Abelard*, Liadin is at base "Protestant" in the sense in which Moore used that word, relying rather on personal integrity than on external discipline as a test for her actions: she takes the enforced vow of the priests, but she knows that she cannot be bound at heart, and plans to keep her tryst with Curithir. Her death from the fall is obviously a tragic accident in the original, but in Moore's retelling it may be a suicide, particularly in view of the fact that when Moore uses the scene again in *Ulick and Soracha*, Soracha's death is obviously the result of her own decision (and it was not long before this that Moore had outraged his brother by asserting in print that their father's death had been a suicide). In *Hail and Farewell* Moore excused his borrowings by saying that the artist finds his materials where he can. Quite so. But it is an argument at least as applicable to the craft of the traditional storyteller, a craft which Moore had consciously or unconsciously adopted some considerable time before *A Story-Teller's Holiday*. Hence in this attempt to add some life and polish to the old stories Moore is not so much adding a foreign and extraneous interest to an uncorrupted original as participating in the very process by which such stories were produced in the first place.

As early as *A Drama in Muslin* Moore detected an analogy between the refusal of normal sexuality by the Church and actual perversion, and from this equation one can construct a long tradition from the pious of doubtful sexuality, beginning with Cecelia Cullen, running through John Norton and Agnes Lahens, and concluding with Joseph of Arimathea. For a man who was often taken to be a scandalous figure, Moore was surprisingly intolerant of homosexuality, a vice which he considered "unnatural"; and this is perhaps the key to his deformed heroes, who are attracted to a religion which is also unnatural, in the sense of actively at variance with normal human instincts. Most of the stories in this book existed in one form or another before the retouching applied by Moore's hand, but the principle of selection involved in their admission to the collection seems almost to make *A Story-Teller's Holiday* an extension of *Celibates*. (Indeed when Moore revised *Celibates* as *Celibate Lives* in 1927, he included "Albert Nobbs," a story composed for *A Story-Teller's Holiday.*) The grotesque test which is intended to control the sensual feelings of Liadin and Curithir is, to a modern mind anyway, already a form of twisted sensuality in itself, and very likely the detail that first drew Moore's attention to the story. That it is not a stray motif in the total plan of the book as a whole may be judged from the prominence accorded to the same test in the next story.

In an anecdote significant of what is to come in the rest of his tale, Alec recalls a time when there were no wolf-dogs in Ireland fit to breed with the only old bitch left from the depredations of the wolves at the monastery of Bregen. A monk named Marban is sent with three breeding dogs from Spain to repair the defect, although, as it turns out, his virility is to be as much on trial as the vigor of his foreign dogs. Wandering at night in the forest of West Mayo, he is glad to see the light of a nunnery, where he asks for food. To his surprise the abbess is glad to see him, even at such a late hour and while she is in an apparent state of undress (the hounds are less dull than Marban, for they immediately begin to sniff at her feet). Before long the same proposal is made to Marban as was made to Curithir and Liadin by the hermit, but with the difference that Marban is to earn merit by lying successively with all the nuns, beginning on the first night with the abbess. Sanctity and authority both presumably come with age, for the abbess presents little temptation to the weary monk after walking forty miles through tough country behind three eager dogs. But in the following nights Marban finds his companions to be younger and more fetching, until he is overcome by the beauty of Luachet, the youngest of the nuns, and with her he is occupied by other things than the counting of rosary beads. When the neighboring abbot is summoned to deal with the scandal, Marban offers the defence that he was following his heart and that, after all, "aren't we more sure that God made our hearts than of anything else?" It is a good argument from Moore's point of view, yet in its intentionalism a "Protestant" argument; and it finds little favor at the convent. The lovers leave together, but without the wolf-dogs, a detail of practical as well as symbolic importance, for they are torn to pieces by wolves on their journey.

Alec now turns to the story of Ligach, the nun who thinks of Christ as a physical lover she will meet in heaven. But, as she is afraid that she will lose her faith unless she is given some sign concerning this distant tryst, the priest Moling is at pains to devise a plan that will accommodate her pious wish. Stripping himself, he climbs onto the cross in the chapel to take the part of Christ. Ligach is overcome, indeed, so much so that Moling gets down to console her abundant tears; in the common excitement of the moment, however, Moling exceeds the requirements of his original role, with the result that, before very much time has elapsed, she is his bride in more than a symbolic union. Quite properly, Moling is not inclined to waste time on blaming himself for a natural lapse, especially since his intention was to save a soul, but he is prudent enough to keep his transgression to himself. Before long Ligach begins to manifest all the signs of pregnancy, a wonder to her, because she believes she has had only a mystical experience, and a still greater wonder to the other nuns, who begin to speak of a miracle. The mysteriously conceived child is called "God's Grandson" in that he is thought to be the son of the Son of God, and there promises to be a new heresy in Ireland until the bishop condemns the new doctrine from the pulpit, interpreting the case in terms of Moling's recent disappearance as an evident sin between a priest and a nun. In an interesting coda to this story, Alec says that the unfortunate child, later named Martin Luther, goes off to Germany, marries a nun, and founds his own religion, itself "no better than a whore."

Alec's conclusion here is an attempt to pass over the evident sensuality of the story to Protestantism, ignoring the clear analogy with the traditional Catholic account of the virgin birth which Moore sees as an old core myth of the religious mind. When Moore responds to Alec's invitation to tell a story of his own choosing, he offers the tale of Lilith from the *Talmud*, for in this account once again there is the ancient Judaeo-Christian fear of sexuality as the

original sin which angers the inhuman Jehovah (even when presenting a story narrated in his own person the novelist holds to the
line of the other stories, for in apparent sympathy with the religious
mind he is investigating, he depicts sex as a blasphemous transgression. There are other, minor matters of detail which indicate the
careful attempt to dovetail this story with the others, as, for example, the pool which Adam, like the hermits, uses to quell his passions).

Moore was always fascinated with the religious mind, but in his
later works there is an observable difference in treatment of this
subject from that to be found in his first works. Cecelia Cullen from
A Drama in Muslin and John Norton from *A Mere Accident* are
conceived of as psychological types, drawn to a preoccupation with
the future life because of their plain inability to cope with this
world, particularly with its demands for normal sexual relationships.
But in 1893 Moore read a book titled *Lettres Portugaises*, supposedly written by a nun but in reality by a seventeenth century
French author by the name of Guilleragues, in which it is clear that
one does not give up one's sexuality with the closing of the convent
door. The first fruit of this reading was the sympathetic portrait of
Evelyn in *Evelyn Innes* and *Sister Teresa*; henceforth the focus is not
on personal, but on institutional, perversity. Normal human beings
are seen as trapped by the life-hatred of religious piety, which
makes "sinners" out of Marban or Moling because they behave in a
perfectly human way when confronted with a "temptation" which it
would be inhuman to resist. Often in his later handling of such
matters Moore is apt to reverse this valuation, making heroes of the
characters who refuse the standards of the conventional devout, in
much the same fashion that he made a moral heroine of Esther
Waters after her "transgression." Certainly the prime example of
such a deliberately unconventional view of religious life is to be
found in Moore's next novel, *Héloise and Abelard*, which unites his
most famous lover in the same person as one of his last fictional
nuns.

III   Héloise and Abelard

Moore knew the story of Héloise and Abelard long before he
undertook to write a book about the doomed lovers of the twelfth
century; nevertheless, he found it necessary to do considerable research on the philosophy and history of the period, ending by

knowing the subject as well as a storyteller must who endeavors to create of the familiar something new and valuable in the retelling. In taking this approach to the events of a historical period he was transforming his technique of the moral delineation of a country, as in his Irish books, to the moral delineation of an epoch. Noting that the old influence of Walter Pater from *Marius the Epicurean* can be detected in the act of sympathetic re-experiencing of the past in this novel and *Aphrodite in Aulis* and *Ulick and Soracha*, critics have not so easily found a category for Moore's final product, whatever attitude it may take to history. Brushing aside analogies with Walter Scott and William Morris inherent in the term "historical romance," Moore gave a clear idea of his view of the magnitude as well as the kind of his achievement in his claim that *Paradise Lost* and *Héloise and Abelard* comprise two of the only three epics in the English language (the third, he thought, is *The Brook Kerith*). Frustrated readers, who may find nothing in common between *Paradise Lost* and *Héloise and Abelard* except a concern with one great sin, perhaps ought to console themselves with the thought that many of Moore's major achievements fit only uneasily into traditional genres, and that this is especially true of the later works, which resemble nothing so much as other late works by George Moore.

While it would not be true at all to say that *Héloise and Abelard* is a translation (a task Moore was to undertake with *The Pastoral Loves of Daphnis and Chloe*), it is incontestable that on commencing this work the novelist was confronted with an existing masterpiece, or rather two masterpieces, Abelard's *Historia Calamitatum* and the collection of letters that makes up the correspondence of the separated lovers. Much actual material in the same words is introduced from the sources into the novel; and in the roughest terms it is possible to say that, in part, there is an act of collaboration taking place between Moore and the original versions comparable with the relationship between the traditional storyteller and his sources. One reason Moore may have been willing to give himself to such a collaboration is that, in the medieval original, a great deal that is characteristic of George Moore already existed. Abelard in his espousal, and Héloise in her practice, of the theory of intentionalism, are "Protestants" in Moore's sense, testing their actions by their own motives rather than by external authority. Héloise's famous comment that though she is guilty, she is also innocent is a statement of such a curious psychological complexion that it allies her with Moore's complicated heroines Grania, Evelyn Innes, and Soracha (once again Moore is apter in his delineation of his heroine in this novel than of the hero). Abelard, too, seems to have his avatars among previous Moore heroes, for the view taken in *Historia Calamitatum* that his liaison is a sort of temptation, leading him away from his mission, is precisely that adopted by Jasper Dean, from *The Bending of the Bough*, John Reid, from *The Strike at Arlingford*, and Diarmuid, from *Diarmuid and Grania* when they begin to fall in love. Again, Abelard's attempt to sublimate Héloise's now unattainable love for him after his castration into a symbolic love of Christ as bridegroom does fit into a traditional religious iconography; but it is an iconography keenly explored by Moore in all his works about the religious life, particularly *Sister Teresa* and *A Story-Teller's Holiday*.

While working on *Héloise and Abelard* Moore complained to an acquaintance that he was trying to avoid "dramatic" situations, a tantalizing remark since in conception much of the book seems either like flattened-out drama, with much of the dialogue converted into meditation and indirect discourse, or, on the contrary, as if the long but essential philosophical discussions of the original have been deliberately broken up into credible, colloquial speaking parts for human beings whose attitude to their beliefs is passionate and as naturally habitual as the air they breathe. It has been pointed out that there is a clear relationship between this book and the treatment of character and dramatic effect in Moore's often-neglected plays; and this is especially true of *Diarmuid and Grania*, a piece concerned with the same basic theme of abduction, wandering, and final separation. As in the play, there is a curious reversal in this novel of abduction, for both make the woman the active, passionate figure and the man the somewhat reluctant victim of the untidy situation into which his love has led him; in both there is an equivalence between the natural emotions aroused by surrender to the love affair and the free life of the birds and animals in the open air; in both the heroine is given to fatalism at decisive moments, as she refuses to make any choice but what the actual minute suggests; and correspondingly both heroes, Diarmuid and Abelard, are never quite sure that they are loved more for their own sake than for their eminent positions, the one as a warrior, the other as a philosopher. Abelard's remark to Héloise, "it seems that I have had you in my mind always," recalls a similar comment by Diarmuid, "I made a

bargain with this brown hair before the beginning of time. . . ,"
which Moore had acquired through Yeats (actually a translation of a
line from Hafiz's *Divan*). Finally, when Héloise's servant, Madelon,
speaks of her own seduction, and the suggestion that she should
have slept with a sword between her and her lover as "in the old
stories," the reference is to Diarmuid and Grania, who were supposed to employ this stratagem in token that they were not actually
making love. The similarities between this play and the novel are
striking enough, but without doubt there are similarities with other
of Moore's works as well, the point being that the storyteller brings
as much to his material as he uses of it; Moore realized with greater
clarity than most writers that what lends the essential interest to any
narrative is the sensibility of the man who perceives and reconsti-
tutes the ingredients into his own uniquely flavored recipe.

The novel opens not with the lovers, but with Phillipe and Fulbert, the father and brother of Héloise, about to part because Phillipe is going to participate in the Crusades, leaving his wife and
daughter behind. In this abandonment Phillipe is already logically a
celibate, in Moore's sense (the role of Peter the Hermit, a prominent celibate, in provoking the Crusades is hinted a number of
times), and a forerunner of Abelard, who sees clearly enough that
success in philosophy means the ruthless discountenancing of family
ties. Phillipe resembles Abelard in one other respect, too, because
he eloped with Héloise's mother, Jeanne, who sacrificed the promise of a great future marriage in order to escape with the young
doctor who had been welcomed into the household.

After the death of both parents Héloise is left perforce to the care
of her uncle Fulbert, a canon of the cathedral, and to the servant
Madelon, who always looks upon herself as "his niece's mother." In
this grotesque distortion of the family, Héloise's career is already
evident, torn as she is between the influence of the canon, a man
comfortable in a celibate life protected from all change, and the
more accessible Madelon, a girl who came from Brittany after giving
birth to an illegitimate child (Héloise's own child, Astrolabe, will
also be born in Brittany). Even at this stage, Fulbert is planning
convent career for his niece because of his sentiment that outside
religious life there is nothing but anxiety; dispatching the child to
the nuns at Argenteuil, he does not visit Héloise at all, informing
her only by letter of the news when certain proof of her father's
death arrives from the Holy Land. Moore makes Fulbert a dry,

bloodless, old man, cast in a more malicious Balzacian mold than the sources, but an interesting scene is devoted to an apparition in which Fulbert seems to be visited by his dead brother, to whom he gives certain promises to take an interest in Héloise's welfare. In this promise to a dead man not only is a motive supplied for Fulbert's otherwise inexplicable grief at the abduction of his niece, a girl for whom he obviously entertains the most moderate affections, but also the overture to the long development of the theme of life paying reverence to death, a theme to be found equally in Moore's familiar picture of religious longing for the consummation of death and Héloise's final acceptance of the sad fact that if she is to be reunited with Abelard at all, it can only be when her life is over.

Recalling Héloise to Paris so that she can make a fair choice between the world and the convent, Fulbert throws open his library to the surprisingly capable girl, supposing that she will begin to read Vergil at the story of Dido and Aeneas. Dido, from whom Aeneas is torn by the will of the gods, is a good likeness of Héloise as she will become in the days to come; but Héloise is more captivated by the quality of life in the age depicted in the epic: eventful, unpredictable, undefined by theories, the classical age seems to her to offer a striking contrast to the ethos of convent life with its insistence that everything be ordered and changeless.

A keen dialectician himself, the canon often holds dinners at his house at which frequently occur fierce discussions about the relations of the persons of the Trinity, a subject of no little importance, since many of Abelard's problems will arise because of his unorthodox views of this matter. (There is still greater relevance if one considers Moore's evident relish at the purely sexual interpretation of this core religious myth in "God's Grandfather" from *A Story-Teller's Holiday*. Many of the unfortunate relationships in *Héloise and Abelard* involve the interposition of a third person into a union which ought to involve only two—Philippe, Jeanne, Jeanne's mother; Margherita, Count Raymond, Mattieu de Rodeboeuf; Geoffrey de Camborne, Flamietta, Gérard de Montador.) The new theories of Peter Abelard are frequently brought up in these discussions, and Héloise begins to perceive a new influence in the world quite different from that of the older philosophers she has heard spoken of.

Abelard's teaching is ruthless in its refusal to rely on past authority, and he wins his way with such energy that Héloise is reminded of the words from *Medea*, "new worlds shall be discovered in the age to come," an association with peculiar force for the young girl, who has come to compare herself to Medea, a woman with two teuil and the contrary impulse to act impulsively like her mother, or sires, the wish to remain safe and changeless like the nuns at Argenteuil and the contrary impulse to act impulsively like her mother or Dido, or Madelon, Héloïse, though for a while temporarily passive, is gradually brought to the point of decision. These characterological choices for Moore's protagonists are always initiated by some change of environment, choices signalled in *Confessions of a Young Man* by the successive transplantings to Paris and London, but here by the move from the convent to the excitement of life in Paris at a time of intellectual enthusiasm. The choice for Héloïse (and for many of Moore's heroes) is between a more or less ordered Apollonian atmosphere where all is predictable and personal experiences count for very little, and a Dionysian life of new encounters, which of its nature is inevitably disorderly in some sense or other. In the Nietzschean coloring given to this sort of decision, Moore is possibly betraying his reading of the German philosopher (whom he certainly did know, for there are specific citations in *Memoirs of My Dead Life* and *Evelyn Innes*), but he is just as likely extrapolating from his own life choices, since the poems and autobiographies betray the same fascination with the root alternatives of human experience as that developed in *Héloïse and Abelard*.

On first hearing Abelard lecture in public Héloïse betrays the peculiar fusion of passion and intellectual acuity which so distinguishes her sensibility: overcome with the relentless progress of his reasoning, she throws herself at his feet and kisses his hand. Yet in her admiration of his philosophical ability she is attracted by that aspect least susceptible to humane considerations, since Abelard is described as a pitiless logician "who cares for nothing but his art." The note of caution which ought to be drawn from Fulbert's description, when coupled with the anecdote of the young Abelard who gave up his lands in Brittany and left his relatives behind so that he might be "free" to study and to teach, means that Abelard can only be a man tied to a specific relationship if he discards his self-chosen mission as a philosopher. (Héloïse is making the same sort of mistake here as that made by Grania, of *Diarmuid and Grania*, who is so overcome by the exploits of Diarmuid that she makes him come away with her, not realizing that in forcing Diarmuid to live a domesticated life as a sheep-farmer she is depriving him of the very heroic characteristics that attracted her in the first place.) The test of this rule of conduct soon follows, for in the lecture that immediately follows his first kiss of Héloise, Abelard finds that his discourse is much less adequate during the disputation, his head being filled with love songs and flute accompaniments.

Moore used an unusually free treatment of the source materials in providing Abelard with a career as a troubador before his days as a teacher; and the novelist defended this freedom as necessary to lend contrapuntal color to a plot otherwise unrelieved in its narrative severity. But there is another side to be considered in this story of the wandering musician, since generally in Moore's works physical journeying is associated with a voyaging of spirit: Abelard, beneath his official, philosophical role, has another self, keenly emotional and active, threatening at any moment to upset his chosen task in life. In this, of course, he is not unlike Héloise, and one needs to balance Héloise's remark to Abelard, "there is a philosopher and a poet in thee, and both seeking for rivalry," with the later observation by Abelard's sister Denise, that he has found his own image and likeness in meeting Héloise. Just as the catastrophic reaction in Kate Ede is only catalyzed, not caused, by her meeting with Dick Lennox, so these lovers are overcome by overwhelming forces whose sources lie within themselves; it is the inner doubleness of their natures that ruins the pair, for it forces them to follow incompatible desires—philosopher and lover, wife and nun, gleeman and dialectician.

Abelard has been living at the canon's house for Héloise's instruction, but when rumors begin to fly he is forced to seek other lodgings, finding, however, that his life is not as placid and predictable as formerly, that, in fact, it has taken on the eventful and abrupt quality of the life Héloise had admired in the picture of classical times from the story of Dido and Aeneas. Seeing that Héloise is pregnant, the two contrive an escape dressed—significantly—as a friar and a nun. As they wander through the forest they meet a wolf-hunter with news of the wolves plaguing the area, and the detail recalls the wolf early in the novel which was speared one winter day as it tried to enter Héloise's door. Wolves seem related in a general way to the unrestrained, natural life of lovers, who live under a double threat, that from their own desires, which can tear them to pieces, just as the wolves who attack the unrequited lover

Jean Guiscard, and that from the restrictive and unsympathetic world, which can no more countenance such deviant behavior than it can the wolves themselves. In a specific way wolves seem to be particularly associated with Abelard, who is clearly prefigured by the wolf mortally wounded as it tries to penetrate into Héloise's house, and who claims that he is treated by his enemies as "a hunted animal." Moore had used this motif before, in connection with Marban from *A Story-Teller's Holiday*, killed by wolves after his passions get the better of him at the convent, and with Diarmuid, in *Diarmuid and Grania*, who claimed that his life with Grania has trapped him "like a wolf in a pit." In all these cases the symbolism is constant.

Abelard returns to Paris, while Héloise remains in Brittany for her confinement; it is in Paris that Abelard discovers that his affair has been regarded by his students as a betrayal of philosophy: "For a thousand years the world has waited, since Plato and Aristotle, and now you would throw God's gift aside for a girl's face. . . . Jesus had no wife, Paul had none, nor had Buddha, but Socrates had, and we know the trouble and ridicule that she brought upon him. . . ." Thirty years and longer spent in writing stories and novels about celibates lie behind these lines, and one would think that no mind but Moore's could have conceived them, were it not for some very similar ideas expressed by Abelard in the *Historia Calamitatum*. At all events the students are to have their wishes fulfilled in a decisive way, since Fulbert, incensed at what he sees as an abandonment of Héloise, hires cutthroats who castrate Abelard, thus removing all impediments to a career in philosophy.

This is the point at which Moore originally intended to end the story, but in fact the conclusion is more than two hundred pages away, for the rest of the account is spent in relating the experiences of Héloise, now retired to a convent so as not to interfere with the vocation of her husband and wholly ignorant of the mishap which renders their relationship no more than symbolic. Two hundred pages in the course of which nothing of any weighty consequence happens is variously a *tour de force* or narrative blunder, depending on one's point of view, but at all times the pace of *Héloise and Abelard* is leisurely, breaking off on occasion for meditations contained in sentences fully two pages long or a page devoted to the resemblance between swallows in their evening flight and bats. But a peculiar virtue of this slowly flowing style is its comprehensiveness, for it is able to embrace all the countless anecdotes of luckless lovers, abducted daughters, and wounded men and animals which clearly and abundantly reflect the main course of the story as it ripples by. And into this is woven the historical material which amplifies, not bloats the text, since the deluded Crusaders who, for an idea, ruthlessly kill entire families of men, women, and children, occupy a contrapuntal relationship with those who, for the sake of philosophy or other fixed notions, bring Abelard and Héloise to their sad end.

IV *Summation*

The Irish Literary Renaissance at the beginning of this century produced some work of extraordinary quality in the writings of James Joyce and W. B. Yeats, much that was frankly miscellaneous in the standard of its attainment, and a great deal of permanent interest only for its historical attachments. In this the Irish Renaissance resembles all movements, for the ability to sustain the highest levels of achievement depends upon individual genius rather than a historical movement. While few would argue that George Moore's work makes him the equal of Yeats or Joyce, yet it remains true that his overall distinction ought to place him very high in the pantheon of a literary school marked by only a few central figures of consummate merit. On the whole, it seems fair to say that Moore has not arrived at his proper place in popular or critical estimate, for although his life and the influences on his work have been subjected to considerable scrutiny, his novels remain largely unread.

Not many writers have enjoyed the kind of technical influence on the work of other writers that Moore possessed in the early years of this century. Profound influences can be detected in the work of such different novelists as James Joyce and Arnold Bennett, and more diffusive tokens of literary inheritance may be discerned in the writing of Virginia Woolf, Mary Lavin, and others. But none of this is an effective substitute for the varied and appreciative readership that Moore's works deserve and will, in the course of time, inevitably acquire.

Going by publishing figures alone, the reader finds that Moore's popularity declined with the general public in proportion as his reputation increased as a "Grand Old Man" of English letters. Perhaps in the long run the fact that his readership was concentrated among writers will preserve his importance far more effectively than a transitory impression created by best-sellers. Arnold Bennett, for example, in his newspaper articles and in his private journals recalled on many occasions his respect for the older novelist. But it is to Bennett's novels that one must go if one wishes to find the fruit of this influence. Bennett, of course, was from the Pottery District of Staffordshire, an area treated with considerable force in Moore's novel *A Mummer's Wife*. Now this one novel contains the germ of ideas and techniques that were to remain with Bennett throughout a long and productive career: the theme of a girl of narrow and restrictive existence who is suddenly exposed to the appeal of an imaginative side of life she has never experienced is adapted from Moore and developed in Bennett's important novels *The Old Wives Tale* and *Anna of the Five Towns*. With both writers, too, inherited beliefs and traditions can seem like a prison as limiting as the smoky confines of the Pottery towns; and indeed both Moore and Bennett make equations between the spiritual limitations of creed and the material limitations of urban squalor. What Bennett most of all owes to Moore is the combination of sense of fact and psychological insight characteristic of the Irish writer's best early novels. Ironically, Moore was done with this period of his career by the time he finished *Esther Waters* in 1894. But Bennett continued to rewrite the central themes of *A Mummer's Wife* until well on into the 1930s.

Even Oscar Wilde, never an admirer of Moore as a man, seems to have used the grammar of art spelled out by Moore in *A Modern Lover*. Lewis Seymour, the central figure of *A Modern Lover*, is essentially an appreciator rather than a creator of art. Despite his obvious personal failures of character he succeeds startlingly with women because he is able to channel into life the charm and imagination he cannot use in art. In all this Lewis Seymour anticipates the hero of Wilde's *The Picture of Dorian Gray*, a novel which also examines the relationship between life and art. Basil Hallward, the true artist in Wilde's novel, is a rather commonplace person outside the act of creation. Like the "Moderns" in Moore's book, he concentrates upon essentials, focussing his will entirely upon his art and not upon the superficial details of dress and manners which occupy so much of Dorian's time. *A Modern Lover* is not a better novel than *The Picture of Dorian Gray*. But it is likely that Wilde would not have written his work in quite the same way if it were not for Moore's example.

Cases could be multiplied of Moore's influence, plain and subtle, upon other writers of the twentieth century. But perhaps the greatest debt the modern writer owes him is the technique known as "stream of consciousness." The stream-of-consciousness technique is a device by which the writer attempts to render the internal transactions of the mind contemplating life rather than depicting the details of the objects outside the mind; it is more interested in the thoughts of a man about his watch than it is about the ticking of the watch itself. Technically it relies upon suspending as far as possible the use of framing words such as "said" or "thought" in favor of direct access to the thoughts in the order in which they are imagined to take place in the mind. Perhaps the best examples of this technique are to be found in the work of James Joyce and Virginia Woolf. Moore came across the use of this technique first in the work of the French writer Edouard Dujardin, who attempted in his book *Les Lauriers sont Coupés* to approximate in prose the uninterrupted musical structure of Wagner's operas. Only in a secondary way did Dujardin think of the psychological usefulness of this technique; and Moore's enthusiasm for the rhythmic and uninterrupted flow of prose as a means of indicating the flow of the mind is an act of adaptation that amounts to a discovery in itself. Excited by this discovery, Moore continued to apply it throughout his subsequent career, and all his novels after about 1887 bear some marks of its use. Moore never used the stream-of-consciousness technique in the extreme form developed by James Joyce for *Ulysses,* but once again the invention of this form in English belongs in the first instance to Moore.

George Moore lived at a time when enormous changes were taking place in English fiction. As a channel for the best French novelists to make their mark upon the English novel, or as a member of the Irish Renaissance in the company of Yeats and Joyce, Moore would already be an important figure. But his importance is more than transitional on the one hand or due to his membership in a group, however notable, on the other. If George Moore had not lived, English literature in the twentieth century would be quite different from what it now is: his influence on other writers has changed the way we think about the novel; and his own work has been of a level of achievement to make it last as long as the English novel will last.

Notes and References

Chapter Two

1. George Moore, *Pagan Poems* (London: Newman and Company, 1881), p. 12.
2. Edwin Gilcher, *A Bibliography of George Moore* (De Kalb: Northern Illinois University Press, 1970), p. 5.
3. Malcolm Brown, *George Moore: A Reconsideration* (Seattle: University of Washington Press, 1955), p. 79.
4. *Confessions of a Young Man*, ed. Susan M. Dick (Montreal: McGill-Queen's University Press, 1972), p. 107.
5. Janet Egleson Dunleavy, *George Moore: The Artist's Vision, The Storyteller's Art* (Lewisburg: Bucknell University Press, 1973), p. 55.
6. *Modern Painting* (London: Walter Scott, 1898), p. 29.
7. Ibid. p. 48.
8. Ibid. p. 228.
9. Jean C. Noël, *George Moore, L'homme et l'oeuvre* (Paris: Didier, 1966), p. 88.
10. Dunleavy, p. 55.
11. Joseph Hone, *The Life of George Moore* (New York: Macmillan, 1936), p. 96.

Chapter Three

1. Hone, p. 85.
2. Hone, p. 139.
3. Hone, p. 141.
4. Dunleavy, p. 97.
5. Dunleavy, p. 102.
6. Helmut E. Gerber, *George Moore in Transition* (Detroit: Wayne State University Press, 1968), p. 93.
7. Stuart P. Sherman, *On Contemporary Literature* (New York: 1917), p. 47.
8. Arthur Schopenhauer, *The Wisdom of Life*, ed. T. Bailey Saunders (London: Swan Sonnenschein, 1890), p. xv.

161

9. Richard Ellmann, *James Joyce* (New York: Oxford University Press, 1965), p. 260.

10. Gerber, p. 115.

Chapter Four

1. William F. Blissett, "George Moore and Literary Wagnerism," *Comparative Literature*, XIII (Winter, 1961), 52–71.

2. Hone, p. 214.

3. Harry Thurston Peck, New York *Bookman* (November, 1901), 260–261.

4. Sister Eileen Kennedy, "Circling Back: The Influence of Ireland on George Moore," unpublished dissertation (Columbia, 1968), p. 103.

Selected Bibliography

PRIMARY SOURCES

Works of George Moore listed in chronological order.

Flowers of Passion. London: Provost & Company, 1878.
Martin Luther: A Tragedy in Five Acts. London: Remington & Company, 1879.
Pagan Poems. London: Newman & Company, 1881.
A Modern Lover. London: Tinsley Brothers, 1883.
A Mummer's Wife. London: Vizetelly & Company, 1885.
Literature at Nurse. London: Vizetelly & Company, 1885.
A Drama in Muslin. London: Vizetelly & Company, 1886.
A Mere Accident. London: Vizetelly & Company, 1887.
Parnell and His Island. London: Swan Sonnenschein, Lowrey & Company, 1887.
Confessions of a Young Man. London: Swan Sonnenschein, Lowrey & Company, 1888.
Spring Days. London: Vizetelly & Company, 1888.
Mike Fletcher. London: Ward & Downey, 1889.
Impressions and Opinions. London: David Nutt, 1891.
Vain Fortune. London: Henry & Company, 1891.
Modern Painting. London: Walter Scott, 1893.
The Strike at Arlingford. London: Walter Scott, 1893.
Esther Waters. London: Walter Scott, 1894.
Celibates. London: Walter Scott, 1895.
Evelyn Innes. London: T. Fisher Unwin, 1898.
The Bending of the Bough. London: T. Fisher Unwin, 1900.
Sister Teresa. London: T. Fisher Unwin, 1901.
The Untilled Field. London: T. Fisher Unwin, 1903.
The Lake. London: William Heinemann, 1905.
Memoirs of My Dead Life. London: William Heinemann, 1906.
The Apostle: A Drama in Three Acts. Dublin: Maunsel & Company, 1911.

163

Hail and Farewell: Ave, Salve, Vale. London: William Heinemann, 1911, 1912, 1914.

Esther Waters: A Play. London: William Heinemann, 1913.

Elizabeth Cooper. Dublin: Maunsel & Company, 1913.

Muslin. London: William Heinemann, 1915.

The Brook Kerith: A Syrian Story. London: T. Werner Laurie, 1916.

Lewis Seymour and Some Women. New York: Brentano's, 1917.

A Story-Teller's Holiday. London: Cumann Sean-eolais na h-Eireann (privately printed), 1918.

Avowals. London: Cumann Sean-eolais na h-Eireann (privately printed), 1919.

The Coming of Gabrielle. London: Cumann Sean-eolais na h-Eireann (privately printed), 1920.

Heloise and Abelard. London: Cumann Sean-eolais na h-Eireann (privately printed), 1921.

In Single Strictness. London: William Heinemann, 1922.

Conversations in Ebury Street. London: William Heinemann, 1924.

Pure Poetry: An Anthology. London: Nonesuch Press, 1924.

The Pastoral Loves of Daphnis and Chloe. London: William Heinemann, 1924.

Daphnis and Chloe, Peronnik the Fool. New York: Boni & Liveright, 1924.

Ulick and Soracha. London: Nonesuch Press, 1926.

Celibate Lives. London: William Heinemann, 1927.

The Making of an Immortal. New York: Bowling Green Press, 1927.

The Passing of the Essenes: A Drama in Three Acts. London: William Heinemann, 1930.

Aphrodite in Aulis. New York: Fountain Press, 1930.

A Communication to My Friends. London: Nonesuch Press, 1933.

Diarmuid and Grania: A Play in Three Acts. Co-written with W. B. Yeats. Edited by Anthony Farrow. Chicago: De Paul, 1974.

1. Letters

Moore Versus Harris. Detroit: privately printed, 1921.

Letters to Dujardin. New York: Crosby Gaige, 1929.

Letters of George Moore. Bournemouth: Sydenham, 1942.

Letters to Lady Cunard. Edited by Rupert Hart-Davis. London: Rupert Hart-Davis, 1957.

George Moore in Transition. Edited by Helmut E. Gerber. Detroit: Wayne State University Press, 1968.

SECONDARY WORKS

ACTON, HAROLD. "George Moore and the Cunard Family." *London Magazine,* V (March 1958), 54–57. An interesting attempt to link the writer to his work.

AIKEN, CONRAD. "The Moorish Arabesque." *Chicago News*, 22 October
   1919, p. 13. One of the first reviews to notice the significance of
   Moore's later style.
ARCHER, WILLIAM. *The Theatrical World of 1893*. London: Walter Scott,
   1894. Compares *The Strike at Arlingford* favorably with Shaw's
   Widower's Houses.
————. *Real Conversations*. London: William Heinemann, 1904. In-
   teresting early recollections.
BATTOCK, MARJORIE. "George Moore." *Dublin Magazine*, XXVII (April–
   June 1952), 27–31. Sees the novels as an attempt to perceive a world
   outside the actual experience of the novelist.
BENNETT, ARNOLD. *Fame and Fiction*. London: Grant Richards, 1901.
   Reserves its strongest praise for the earlier novels, singling out most of
   all *A Mummer's Wife* and *A Drama in Muslin*.
BENSON, E. F. "George Moore." *Spectator*, CL (27 January 1933), 110–
   111. An obituary survey of Moore's importance by a writer who considers that Moore will survive because of his dedication to artistic
   beauty.
BLANCHE, JACQUES ÉMILE. *Portraits of a Lifetime*. New York: Coward
   McCann, 1933. Recollections by one of the few to remember Moore
   from France.
BLISSETT, WILLIAM F. "George Moore and Literary Wagnerism." *Comparative Literature*, XII (Winter, 1961), 52–71. A major study, despite
   its length.
BROWN, MALCOLM. *George Moore: A Reconsideration*. Seattle: University
   of Washington Press, 1955. A lucid and valuable work.
BUCHANAN, ROBERT. "The Modern Young Man as Critic." *University Re-
   view*, III (Jan 1889), 353–72. A curiosity of Victorian prudery in its
   condemnation.
COLLET, GEORGES-PAUL. *George Moore et la France*. Paris: Droz, 1957.
   Solid, not exciting.
CUNARD, NANCY. *GM:Memories of George Moore*. London: Rupert Hart-
   Davis, 1956. Charming recollections.
DICK, SUSAN M., ed. *Confessions of a Young Man*. Montreal: McGill-
   Queen's University Press, 1972. A model of editing and scholarship.
DUNLEAVY, JANET EGLESON. *George Moore: The Artist's Vision, The
   Storyteller's Art*. Lewisburg: Bucknell University Press, 1973. Espe-
   cially valuable for the early novels.
EGLINTON, JOHN. *Irish Literary Portraits*. London: Macmillan, 1935.
ELLMANN, RICHARD. "The Backgrounds of THE DEAD." *The Kenyon
   Review*, XX (Autumn 1958), 507–28. About the influence of *Vain For-
   tune* on Joyce's story.
FERGUSON, WALTER D. *The Influence of Flaubert on George Moore*.
   Philadelphia: University of Pennsylvania Press, 1934.

FREEMAN, JOHN. *A Portrait of George Moore in a Study of His Work.* London: T. Werner Laurie, 1922. An admiring but insufficiently critical work graced by occasional fine insights.

GOODWIN, GERAINT. *Conversations with George Moore.* New York: Knopf, 1930.

HARRIS, FRANK. *Contemporary Portraits.* New York: privately printed, 1919. Unsteady mixture of recollection, fiction, and criticism.

HICKS, GRANVILLE. *Figures of Transition.* New York: Macmillan, 1939.

HONE, JOSEPH M. *The Life of George Moore.* New York: Macmillan, 1936. One of the great biographies of the century.

————. *The Moores of Moore Hall.* London: Jonathan Cape, 1939.

HOUGH, GRAHAM. *The Last Romantics.* London: Gerald Duckworth, 1949. Interesting discussions of Moore's historical position.

HOWARTH, HERBERT. *The Irish Writers 1880–1940.* London: Rockcliff, 1958. Limited but intelligent analyses of Moore and others.

HUGHES, DOUGLAS A. *The Man of Wax: Critical Essays on George Moore.* New York: New York University Press, 1971.

MACCARTHY, DESMOND. *Portraits.* London: Putnam, 1932.

MITCHELL, SUSAN. *George Moore.* Dublin: Maunsel, 1916. Witty, caustic and irreverent study of the man and the works.

MOORE, MAURICE. *An Irish Gentleman: George Henry Moore.* London: T. Werner Laurie, 1913.

MORGAN, CHARLES. *Epitaph on George Moore.* New York: Macmillan, 1935.

NEJDEFORS-FRISK, SONJA. *George Moore's Naturalistic Prose.* Upsala: Lundequist, 1952.

NOEL, JEAN C. *George Moore: l'homme et l'oeuvre.* Paris: Didier, 1966. The most complete study of Moore's life and work.

OWENS, GRAHAM, ed. *George Moore's Mind and Art.* New York: Barnes and Noble, 1970.

STARKIE, ENID. "Rimbaud in England." *Adam International Review,* XXII (Winter 1954), 2–9. Moore seen as an able critic of French poetry (a rare view).

WOLFE, HUMBERT. *George Moore.* London: Shaylor, 1931.

YEATS, W. B. *The Autobiography of W. B. Yeats.* New York: Macmillan, 1965. A useful corrective to the memoirs of George Moore, although frequently as unreliable.

1. Bibliographies

English Literature in Transition, II, 2 (1959), 3–91. The standard secondary bibliography. Supplements in later issues.

GILCHER, EDWIN. *A Bibliography of George Moore.* De Kalb: Northern Illinois University Press, 1970. Unique and indispensable.

Index

Abbey Theatre, 18
Aquinas, Thomas, 118
Augustine, St., 19
Austen, Jane, 76, 80

Balzac, Honore de, 32, 61, 67, 80, 85, 94, 104, 108
Baudelaire, Charles, 23, 24, 28, 31, 99
Beckett, Samuel, 21
Bennett, Arnold, 158–59
Bentham, Jeremy, 74
Blissett, William, 109
Braddon, Mrs., 31
Brillat Savarin, Anthelme, 50
Brown, Malcolm, 29
Byron, Lord, 62

Cabaner, Ernest, 31
Carlyle, Thomas, 32
Catullus, 130
Celtic Twilight, The (Yeats), 17
Churchill, Winston, 22
Cloches de Corneville, Les, 53
Corot, Jean Baptiste, 113
Crawford, Virginia, 104

Defoe, Daniel, 46, 69
Degas, Edgar, 31, 33, 63, 66, 103
Dickens, Charles, 69, 79, 80, 86, 104
Dolmetsch, Arnold, 104
Dujardin, Edouard, 16, 20, 67, 87, 99, 125, 138, 160
Dumas, Alexandre (père), 14
Dunleavy, Janet Egleson, 31, 37, 69
Duruy, Victor, 46

Eden, Sir William, 106
Eglinton, John, 112–13
Eliot, George, 34, 104
Eliot, Thomas Stearns, 21
Ellis, Ashton, 125
Ellmann, Richard, 93
Etty, William, 90

Flaubert, Gustave, 52–53, 88, 94, 102

Gainsborough, Thomas, 90
Gautier, Théophile, 14, 88
Gilcher, Edwin, 29
Gill, T. P., 133, 135
Gregory, Lady, 18, 103, 132, 136

Hafiz, 153
Harland, Henry, 102
Harris, Frank, 79
Hawkins, Lewis Weldon, 14, 31
Historia Calamitatum (Abelard), 150, 157
Hone, Joseph, 65
Hugo, Victor, 64
Huysmans, J. K., 112

Ingres, Jean Auguste, 65
Irish Literary Theatre, The, 18, 103
Irish Renaissance, The, 18–19, 88, 137, 158, 160

James, Henry, 66
James, William, 46
Joyce James, 16, 20, 41, 47, 51, 58, 93–95, 104, 108–109, 123, 129, 137–38, 158, 160
Jullian, M., 14

167

Kafka, Franz, 21
Kant, Immanuel, 39
Kempis, Thomas A., 128

Lady Audley's Secret (Braddon), 31, 62
Lavin, Mary, 158
Lettres Portugaises (Guilleragues), 150
Libraries, Circulating, 15, 30
Lopez, Bernard, 14

Manet, Edouard, 33–34, 38, 63, 135
Martyn, Edward, 17–18, 79, 103, 133–36
Melba, Nellie, 104
Melodic Line, The, 20
Mendès, Catulle, 23, 63
Meyer, Kuno, 147
Meyerfield, Max, 69
Millais, John, 131
Moloney, William, 12
Moore, Augustus, 11, 79
Moore, George Augustus (1852–1933), childhood and education, 11–13; influence of, 158–60; Irish period, 103–37; last novels, 138–60; middle years in London, 17–21, 32–102; Paris experiences, 12–16
WORKS:
Aphrodite in Aulis, 20, 151
Apostle, The, 132, 139
Bending of the Bough, The, 152
Brook Kerith, The, 20, 52, 138–42
Celibates, 25, 93–102, 108, 148
Communication to My Friends, A, 68, 74, 104
Confessions of a Young Man, 14, 29, 31, 59–68, 78–79, 88, 91, 99
Defensio Pro Scriptis Meis, 55
Diarmuid and Grania, 17, 103, 107, 132, 144, 152, 155
Drama in Muslin, A, 17, 28, 52–58, 63, 68–69, 77–78, 85, 103, 144
Esther Waters, 46, 53, 62, 67–79, 86, 93–94
Evelyn Innes, 17, 24, 31, 102–11, 150, 155
Flowers of Passion, 14, 22–26, 28, 70
Hail and Farewell, 14, 19, 24, 29, 31, 65, 78–79, 83, 87, 92, 94, 104, 129–37

Héloise and Abelard, 20, 31, 52, 150–58
Impressions and Opinions, 32, 88
Lake, The, 19, 111, 123–29, 139
Martin Luther, 14
Memoirs of My Dead Life, 29, 155
Mere Accident, A, 67, 77, 79, 85, 93–94
Mike Fletcher, 24, 26, 28, 31, 78, 82–87, 92
Modern Lover, A, 14, 26, 28, 30–45, 62, 66, 68, 79
Modern Painting, 32–34, 90, 95–96, 114
Mummer's Wife, A, 15, 45–51, 53, 85
Pagan Poems, 14, 26–30, 85
Parnell and His Island, 12, 29, 94, 113, 115, 122, 130
Pastoral Loves of Daphnis and Chloe, The, 94, 151
Sister Teresa, 31, 102, 104, 109–12, 150
Spring Days, 26, 31, 78–82, 86, 92, 94
Story Teller's Holiday, A, 143–50, 157
Strike at Arlingford, The, 44, 77, 152
Ulick and Soracha, 20, 147, 151
Untilled Field, The, 17, 19, 93, 112–23, 143
Vain Fortune, 26, 31, 78, 88–93, 94
Moore, George Henry, 11, 13
Moore, John, 11
Moore, Maurice, 11, 103, 134
Morris, William, 21, 151

New English Art Club, 33
Newman, Cardinal, 134
Newton, Isaac, 22
Nietzsche, Friedrich, 155
Noel, Jean, 36

O'Connor, Frank, 137

Pater, Walter, 16, 20, 24, 52, 66–67, 138, 142, 151
Pissarro, Camille, 63, 66
Poe, Edgar Allan, 99

Renan, Ernest, 142
Richardson, Samuel, 69, 127
Rolleston, T. W., 133

Rossetti, Dante Gabriel, 21, 23
Rousseau, Jean-Jacques, 19, 28, 131
Russell, George, 19, 107, 132–33

Saunders, T. Bailey, 86
Schopenhauer, Arthur, 16, 24, 28, 60–61, 70, 73, 76, 80–81, 84, 86–87, 89, 99
Scott, Sir Walter, 151
Scribe, Augustin, 14
Secret Rose, The (Yeats), 17
Shakespeare, William, 61, 104
Shaw, George Bernard, 15, 22, 51, 139, 142
Shelley, Percy Bysshe, 13, 62
Sherman, Stuart, 78
Smollett, Tobias, 127
Stendhal (Marie Henri Bayle), 101
Stephens, James, 143
Sterne, Laurence, 136–37
Stevenson, R. L., 66
Strauss, David, 142
Stream-of-consciousness, 16, 138, 160
Swinburne, A. C., 21, 23–24
Symons, Arthur, 23, 104
Synge, J. M., 143

Talmud, The, 149
Thackeray, W. M., 86, 101
Théatre Libre, 18
Tolstoy, Lev, 30
Trollope, Anthony, 21
Turgenev, Ivan, 16, 67–68, 80, 103–104, 113, 143

Verlaine, Paul, 99
Villon, François, 23, 119
Vizetelly, Henry, 45, 87

Wagner, Richard, 16, 20, 40, 83, 99, 104, 106, 109, 138, 143
Whistler, J. M., 33
Wilde, Oscar, 13, 44, 64, 109, 159
Woolf, Virginia, 21, 138, 158, 160

Yeats, John Butler, 106
Yeats, William Butler, 14, 17–18, 60, 82, 103, 106–108, 122, 130, 132, 134–36, 143, 153, 158

Zola, Emile, 15, 36, 38, 45, 51–52, 61, 67, 79–80, 87, 101